To: _____

From: _____

GOD'S Peace
for When You Can't Sleep

BY CHRISTINA VINSON

THOMAS NELSON
Since 1798

NASHVILLE   MEXICO CITY   RIO DE JANEIRO

Contents

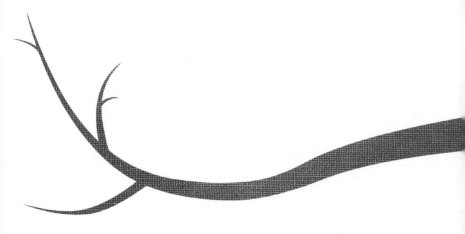

God's Peace for When You Feel Overwhelmed

*I*t's that time of night again. The house is quiet, the stars are shining against the blackened sky, and everyone is asleep. Everyone, that is, except you. Your mind is racing, shoulders still hunched with the day's obligations, fists already clenched with the worries of what a new day will bring. In a word, you're overwhelmed. Exhausted. Wondering when the to-do list will let up, when the financial pressure will finally subside, when your days will feel like less of a rat race.

And so it begins every evening: the endless fight for sleep. As the hours pass, anxiety creeps in with the knowledge morning is drawing closer—and you haven't yet slept. The day is dawning, but rest has only come in intermittent fits. In fact, you're more exhausted than ever while lying in the rumpled mess of your sheets, trying, *trying* to ignore the ticking of the clock. Does this ring true for you right now? Are you letting out a whoosh of relief, thinking, *Yes, I get it. That's me. I am not alone!*

My friend, take heart. For the burdens you are carrying in your heart, mind, and body aren't yours to bear alone. There is One who understands and is waiting to help you.

Again and again, God reminds us in Scripture that through leaning on Him, we will find rest for our souls—our downtrodden, utterly wearied souls. Jesus Christ Himself doesn't just tell us to give Him our burdens; He offers to take our burdens *for us*. He commands us, all of us who are weary and heavy laden, to come to Him and lay our burdens down. Not just half of them, not the ones that seem easily fixable—all of them. What He gives in return is like a cooling, soul-satisfying drink: He gives rest.

As you reflect on these words, on the promises and call of the Lord, take in a deep breath. Exhale the stress you are holding, and breathe in the peace of God, letting the promises of His Word flood your tired soul. And then, as you close your eyes and lay your head down, know that He is right there with you; He is your rock, your strength, your ever-present help in times of trouble, even in the quiet hours of the morning. Cling to that rock!

*"Come to me, all you who are weary and
burdened, and I will give you rest."*

MATTHEW 11:28

*From the ends of the earth I call to you,
I call as my heart grows faint;
lead me to the rock that is higher than I.*

PSALM 61:2

*In peace I will lie down and sleep,
for you alone, LORD,
make me dwell in safety.*

PSALM 4:8

Prayer

LORD, YOU ARE THE GIVER of rest. Help me trust that You have everything under control, and that my job is not to juggle everything, but to hand all of my burdens over to You, the all-powerful, able, strong God.

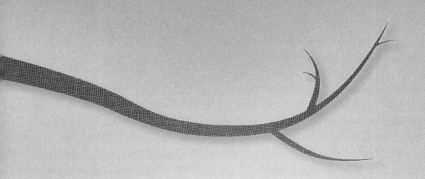

Blessing

MAY GOD'S STRENGTH BE
yours tonight, calming you
with His goodness, nourishing
you with His richness,
satisfying you with His all-
encompassing presence and
grace. May your burdens be
replaced with joy and your
worries exchanged for peace.

Praise

I PRAISE YOU, LORD, FOR

taking my burdens over

and over, never ceasing

to lighten my load.

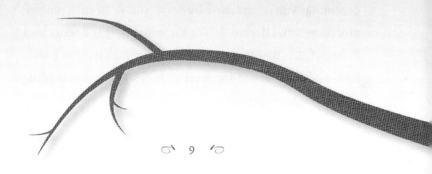

God's Peace for When You Are Angry

When you are angry, it can be difficult to fall asleep. You lie in bed stewing, your mind constantly replaying the events that led to your anger. Maybe it was something that happened today: your coworker's criticism, your child's rebellious behavior, the church member's gossip with you at the center. Or maybe something happened in the past but continually comes back to the surface of your mind. Her unkind words, his refusal to apologize, the betrayal you never saw coming, the wounds you think will never heal. Those are hard things to forgive—and hard things to let go.

While your day may be filled with so much busyness there's no time to properly contemplate these difficult circumstances, your nights lying in bed are often not that way. All you have is yourself, your pillow, and your thoughts. And when your thoughts turn to these provoking situations, they can lead to long nights of restlessness. Instead of peacefully dreaming, you're troubled by ways you've been wronged, mistreated, and deceived. Not surprisingly, this doesn't lead to peaceful, bliss-filled sleep. Instead, your heart feels a little hard and your desire for revenge keeps knocking, holding your thoughts captive.

What would it look like to let that anger go? The resentment that pounds in your veins and makes your face flush with frustration is really controlling *you*—not the person who wronged you, not the friend who deceived you, not the spouse who betrayed you. In short, the anger you hold and nurse and keep on simmer is impacting you most fervently. It's stealing your body of rest and festering in the deepest parts of your soul. Be careful, beloved. The enemy relishes the angst you are feeling. But there is good news: the Lord is able to rescue you from it.

In Psalm 37:8, the psalmist said, "Refrain from anger, and forsake wrath! Fret not yourself; it tends only to evil" (ESV). Harboring unforgiveness is not only harmful for you—it's also exhausting. Make a change tonight, even a small change. Cry to God for help. Ask Him for supernatural strength to breathe deeply, inhaling forgiveness and exhaling bitterness. Imagine His loving arms around you, letting you know that He understands. This kind of change doesn't often happen overnight. But just for this night, in these quiet moments, you can take a small step toward change—cleansing, purifying, rest-giving change.

My dear brothers and sisters, take note of this:
Everyone should be quick to listen, slow to speak and
slow to become angry, because human anger does
not produce the righteousness that God desires.

JAMES 1:19–20

Bless those who persecute you; bless and do not curse. . . .
Do not be overcome by evil, but overcome evil with good.

ROMANS 12:14, 21

A gentle answer turns away wrath,
but a harsh word stirs up anger.

PROVERBS 15:1

Prayer

FATHER, HELP ME TAKE A step toward healing and forgiveness tonight. Remind me of the everlasting patience You hold, and help me regard others with the same gracious, loving, Spirit-filled attitude.

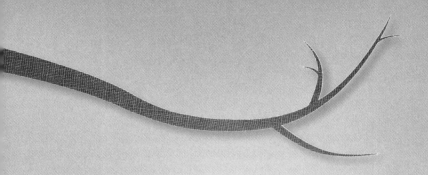

Blessing

TONIGHT, MAY THE
compassion of God the Father
fill your heart and your mind,
may the love of Jesus Christ
permeate your spirit, and
may the tender care of the
Holy Spirit give you peace.

Praise

I PRAISE YOU, MOST
generous Father, for Your
continued mercy toward me
when I fail, never harboring
Your anger against me, but
forever opening Your arms to
embrace me, the prodigal child.

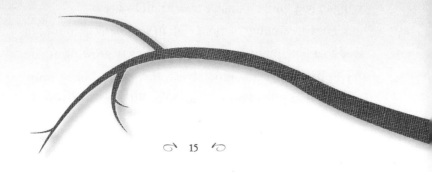

God's Peace for When Your Bank Account Is Empty

*I*nhale, exhale. You try to breathe slowly and deeply, in and out, but the anxiety is still there. Mentally, you tabulate your checking account and envision the stacks of bills on the kitchen table, watching dollar signs flash before your eyes. You are worried about money, or lack of it, and it's keeping you up into the wee hours of the night. Take heart, and listen to these words.

Jesus is very specific in talking about our daily needs. In Matthew 6:25, He commands us with three very specific words: "Do not worry." Then, He lists the things that we tend to worry about—our physical needs: food, drink, and clothing. In our world today, money buys these items. However, there are times when the bills pile up, the money pours out of the bank account like water down the drain, and all of a sudden you're looking at very real, pressing needs and a very small amount of money. That may be why you're lying in bed tonight, unable to drift off to sleep.

The tiny amount of money left in your bank account can lead to a long night of lying awake, anxiety growing as you try to pare down the grocery list, the medical bills—anything to make that bottom line look a little less worrisome.

It's scary, isn't it? Having to rely on a very present—yet also invisible—God for your tangible and physical needs. Will He help you? Will He provide? He gives us the answer in Scripture. Jesus doesn't tell us not to worry—and then not come through on His end! He holds up His end of His promises.

The Lord of your own heart is the same Jehovah-Jireh who provided Abraham a ram to sacrifice instead of his own son (Genesis 22:13). He's the same God who led the Israelites through the Red Sea on dry ground (Exodus 14:21–22), and the same Father who provided manna around the Israelites' campsites (16:13–15). It is so hard to trust when the outlook is bleak and the bills are stacked in piles; it's even harder if you have a family to care for too. But you can rest in the knowledge that your heavenly Father cares for every sparrow, every blade of grass, every hair on your head, and most of all, your every need. He will take care of you. Cast your cares on Him and sleep peacefully tonight—He is with you.

"Therefore I tell you, do not worry about your life, what you will eat or drink; or about your body, what you will wear. Is not life more than food, and the body more than clothes? Look at the birds of the air; they do not sow or reap or store away in barns, and yet your heavenly Father feeds them. Are you not much more valuable than they? Can any one of you by worrying add a single hour to your life?"

MATTHEW 6:25–27

Keep your lives free from the love of money and be content with what you have, because God has said, "Never will I leave you; never will I forsake you." So we say with confidence, "The Lord is my helper; I will not be afraid. What can mere mortals do to me?"

HEBREWS 13:5–6

*Yet he gave a command to the skies above
and opened the doors of the heavens;
he rained down manna for the people to eat,
he gave them the grain of heaven.
Human beings ate the bread of angels;
he sent them all the food they could eat.
He let loose the east wind from the heavens
and by his power made the south wind blow.
He rained meat down on them like dust,
birds like sand on the seashore.*

PSALM 78:23–27

Prayer

LORD, I AM AFRAID. I AM so anxious about money and it's on my mind all hours of the day and night. Please help me trust that You are Jehovah-Jireh, the God who provides for my every need, and grant me rest in the knowledge that You are my helper.

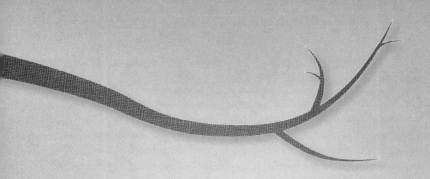

Blessing

MAY YOU DEEPLY KNOW
the care God bestows on
you. May you experience
His provision from dawn
to dusk day after day, and
be filled with thanksgiving
for His good gifts.

Praise

I PRAISE YOU, LORD, FOR

Your rapt attention on my
life. Not a hair falls from my
head without You noticing,
and You promise to never
leave me or forsake me. Thank
You for being my provider!

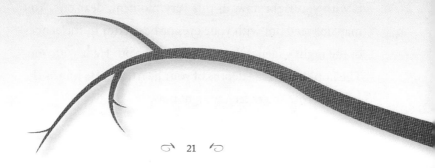

God's Peace for When You Feel Sadness

*A*re you feeling sad right now? Perhaps you are missing someone—a grandparent, a faraway child, a deployed spouse, or a loved one who has passed away. Maybe you're sad about the circumstances in your life: a lost job, a relationship that didn't pan out, or a sick friend. There are countless scenarios, but it's important that you know two truths: you are not alone, and it's okay to feel sad.

You are not alone because your heavenly Father is watching over you. As sure as the stars that twinkle in the night sky, as dependable as the evening tide, He is with you. He's there when you're overflowing with joy as well as when you're overwhelmed with sadness. He is the helper of the helpless, the One who whispers "be still" to life's storms.

Jesus declares He is with you always. And He confirms it with the word *surely*. In Matthew 28:20, He said, "And surely I am with you always, to the very end of the age." He is with you right now, in this very moment, dear one. You may not see Him with your eyes or hear Him in the echoes of the night's silence, but let me assure you: He is with you. The Lord knows the depths of your heart, and He knows the exact sorrow you're feeling right now.

Have faith that as each moment passes, you are getting closer to a break in the clouds. Morning, and its new beginnings, will come—it always does. The rain will stop, the clouds will part, and you will once again find light in your heart. Even if your sadness is not relieved when tomorrow's dawn breaks, it will be washed away eventually, for you serve a God who brings solace and healing to His children—He will bless those who mourn (Matthew 5:4).

Be comforted, dear friend, for the goodness of the Lord will be revealed. Cling to that as you fall asleep tonight. Curl back into bed, pull the covers up, rest your head on your pillow, and know that you are loved extravagantly and beyond measure.

Weeping may stay for the night,
but rejoicing comes in the morning.

PSALM 30:5

For the LORD comforts his people
and will have compassion on his afflicted ones.

ISAIAH 49:13

Because of the LORD's great love we are not consumed,
for his compassions never fail.
They are new every morning;
great is your faithfulness.

LAMENTATIONS 3:22–23

Prayer

LORD, THE SADNESS IN my heart overcomes me in this moment. I desire to see Your goodness, even for a moment, this evening. Please surround me with Your gentle presence, for my heart feels heavy within me.

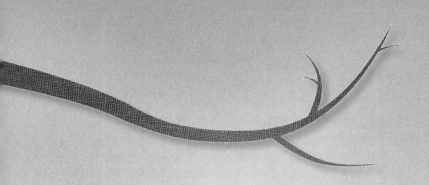

Blessing

MAY YOU EXPERIENCE
the help and renewal of
God your Father. May you
sleep soundly tonight with
the sweet presence of the
Lord enveloping you with
love and reminding you of
His great faithfulness.

Praise

EVEN WHEN I AM
downcast, my heart still longs
to praise You, my God. You are
a great, mighty, and steadfast
Father who cares for His children.
Thank You for abiding with
me in my most difficult times
and most joyous hours. You are
the rock on which I stand.

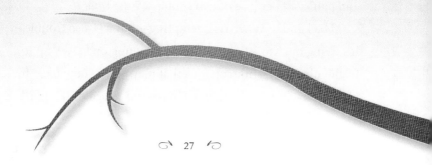

God's Peace for When You Have So Many What-Ifs

The Land of What-Ifs is a tempting place to dwell. It is also a dangerous place to be. And chances are, if you flipped to this page, you're stepping foot into its territory. Before you even pull the covers back, your mind is racing with questions. *What if I choke up during the meeting tomorrow? What if my child is diagnosed with learning disabilities? What if the test result comes back positive? What if I don't get the job?* There are countless "what-if" scenarios, both big and small. But they have one thing in common: they don't help.

While you're lying in bed, trying to gear down for the day, your mind is whirring, spinning every possible negative scenario into a sticky, all-consuming web. You get trapped in it, and spend hours burrowing deeper and deeper—with nothing positive to show for it. In fact, you are so imprisoned in this web that you're paralyzed with fear, anxiety, and panic, all because of two simple words: *what if.*

The Land of What-Ifs is tempting—but it is also trouble. It's living out anxiety in our minds, hyping ourselves up to frightening, stressful scenarios that may never come true. It places ourselves in the role of God—and relegates the Lord

elsewhere. In short, it's a place that Christians need to fight against.

If you're dwelling in the Land of What-Ifs—whether you're a frequent traveler, or have just crossed into its borders—get out now. Ask the Lord to take every thought captive. He can and will do it. He doesn't want us to be filled with anxiety over the what-ifs in life, because He has them all under control. He knows your fears and anxieties—and He wants you to come to Him with them, not let them whirl and swirl in your head, letting you forego sleep for a tromp in dangerous territory. Instead of a blissful night of sleep, you end up on a battleground.

Dear child, come out of that land and dwell in the safety and surety of the Lord's arms. When you are in His presence, nothing can harm you because He is with you. You can let the worries of today—and tomorrow—float away. Stay in the present moment with Him beside you. It's a much better place to be. When you dwell with Him, He will fill you with assurance of His perfect plan for you. He goes before you and prepares a path for you. You don't need to figure everything out; God already has.

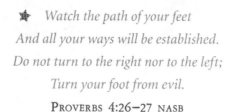

Watch the path of your feet
And all your ways will be established.
Do not turn to the right nor to the left;
Turn your foot from evil.

PROVERBS 4:26–27 NASB

Say to those who have an anxious heart,
"Be strong; fear not!
Behold, your God
will come with vengeance,
with the recompense of God.
He will come and save you."

ISAIAH 35:4 ESV

Do not be anxious about anything, but in everything
by prayer and supplication with thanksgiving let your
requests be made known to God. And the peace of
God, which surpasses all understanding, will guard
your hearts and your minds in Christ Jesus.

PHILIPPIANS 4:6–7 ESV

"Cast all your anxiety on him because he cares for you."

1 PETER 5:7

We take captive every thought to make it obedient to Christ.

2 CORINTHIANS 10:5

Prayer

LORD, I CONFESS THAT
when I am anxious, I am not
fully relying on You. Give me
the courage to let go of my
fears and meager plans, and to
embrace the good, life-giving
plan You have for me.

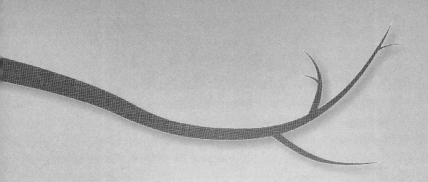

Blessing

MAY YOU KNOW DEEP,
soul-satisfying peace, given
from the One who will
direct your every step.

Praise

GOD, I PRAISE YOU FOR

Your great love. You desire
for me to cast my anxieties on
You so I may live a life full
of peace and joy. Thank You
for taking on my burdens!

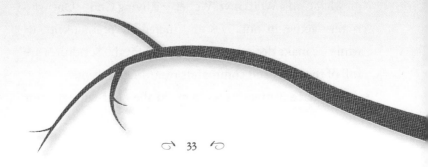

God's Peace for When You Are Facing Big Decisions

*L*ife is full of questions. They range from small to large: *What will I wear today? When will I get groceries? Should I take the job abroad? Is this my future spouse? How do I discipline my child?*

Each decision we make is important in its own way, but big decisions are usually the ones that keep us up at night. Perhaps you are facing a big decision in your life right now, and it's one that's keeping you from any sleep. Along with decisions come results and consequences—sometimes good, and sometimes not so good. You may be worried about the results your decision will bring. Will it be good for your career? Good for your family? Stunting for your spiritual growth? There are so many big things to consider when making decisions.

If you are tossing and turning this evening, overwhelmed with the big decision in front of you, take a moment to reflect on what God's Word says. We serve a living God—One who is very active in our lives and incredibly present with us while we make decisions. And thankfully, the Scriptures are full of thoughts and commands regarding decisions.

Proverbs 3 urges us to "trust in the Lord with all your

heart . . . and he will make your paths straight" (vv. 5–6). It doesn't say to worry about our decisions and it certainly doesn't advocate for sleepless nights. Instead, Scripture continually points us toward the Lord and what He would have us to do. He is the best one to turn to while making decisions, big and small.

In Philippians 4, the apostle Paul urges believers to dwell on things above, things that are lovely and worthy of praise. He specifically said, "Finally, brothers and sisters, whatever is true, whatever is noble, whatever is right, whatever is pure, whatever is lovely, whatever is admirable—if anything is excellent or praiseworthy—think about such things. Whatever you have learned or received or heard from me, or seen in me—put it into practice" (vv. 8–9). Tonight, in the quietness of your home, and in the company of crickets and the occasional car passing by, think about how God is true, honorable, right, pure, and lovely. With this truth, He will lead you in your decision-making. Seek His ways, and He will provide for your every need. He will guide your every step, and His Word will be a lamp unto your feet. Go to sleep knowing that while you sleep, the Lord is preparing a path for you. You will find direction; He will make a way.

*Make me know Your ways, O L*ORD;
Teach me Your paths.
Lead me in Your truth and teach me,
For You are the God of my salvation;
For You I wait all the day.

PSALM 25:4–5 NASB

You make known to me the path of life;
you will fill me with joy in your presence,
with eternal pleasures at your right hand.

PSALM 16:11

But if any of you lacks wisdom, let him ask of
God, who gives to all generously and without
reproach, and it will be given to him.

JAMES 1:5 NASB

I will instruct you and teach you
in the way you should go;
I will counsel you with my loving eye on you.

PSALM 32:8

Praise

I PRAISE YOU FOR YOUR
provision, Almighty God!
You have shown Yourself
faithful each step of my
way, and I am grateful for
a God like You who never
leaves His children, but leads
them, whether with a gentle
whisper or a burning bush.

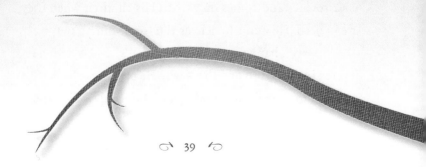

God's Peace for When You Are Anxious

*T*hump, thump, thump. That's the sound of your heart, beating erratically and quickly, reminding you of the anxiety that's building up in your body. You can feel your body tense, your palms start to sweat, and the familiar dread kick in: you're panicking.

Oh, my friend. Whether you're struggling with anxiety and panic attacks, or you are anxious about current circumstances in your life, it all can feel very overwhelming. You may not be sure if you can survive even this hour because you feel so alone. You may feel very lonely right now, in solitude with your thoughts and your mind that won't stop racing, in a body that feels very foreign and charged and rather scary.

The Lord is near. That is a promise. He is with you. Even as your heart races uncontrollably, His presence fills your room. He is not judging you or berating you for not trusting Him enough—the Holy Spirit is interceding for you. He is your rescuer and comes quickly to His children when they are in need. He wants to deliver you from your anxiety.

Anxiety is hard. God knows this. That's why He addresses it often in His Word and that's why He promises His perfect presence in the Bible. In Philippians 4:6, Paul says, "Do not

be anxious about anything, but in every situation, by prayer and petition, with thanksgiving, present your requests to God." As you wrestle with your anxiety right now, picture yourself writing every worry down and handing the list over to God. He wants to take the list from you. Paul goes on to say that when we give our anxieties to the Lord, something amazing happens: "And the peace of God, which transcends all understanding, will guard your hearts and your minds in Christ Jesus" (Philippians 4:7).

Sometimes anxiety relates to specific worries, but other times it rears its ugly head with no warning signs, no triggers, and no reason. It's okay; you are not alone. The Lord is available at all times. In Psalm 34, David experienced the Lord's deliverance and he praised God afterward, saying, "I sought the Lord, and he answered me; he delivered me from all my fears." He can deliver you too. He knows what you need. Breathe in and out slowly; breathe in His promises and truths, and breathe out the fear and anxiety that's riveted deep in your soul. Even as you drift to sleep, He will not leave: the Lord will watch over your coming and going both now and forevermore.

The righteous cry out, and the Lord *hears them;*
he delivers them from all their troubles.
The Lord *is close to the brokenhearted*
and saves those who are crushed in spirit.
The righteous person may have many troubles,
but the Lord *delivers him from them all;*
he protects all his bones,
not one of them will be broken.

PSALM 34:17–20

The God of my rock; in him will I trust: he is my
shield, and the horn of my salvation, my high tower,
and my refuge, my savior; thou savest me from
violence. I will call on the Lord, *who is worthy to be*
praised: so shall I be saved from mine enemies.

2 SAMUEL 22:3–4 KJV

You are my hiding place;
you will protect me from trouble
and surround me with songs of deliverance.

PSALM 32:7

Prayer

ABBA, FATHER. I AM SO full of anxiety and I don't know what to do except turn to You. Your Word says to give my requests to You, so I'm asking You to please come to my rescue, deliver me from all of my distress, and comfort me under the shadow of Your wings.

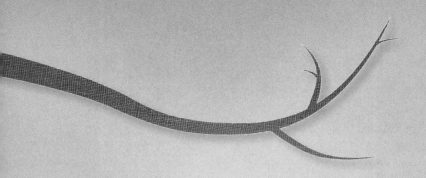

Blessing

DEAR CHILD OF GOD,

may you experience the
love of Christ more deeply
than you have ever felt, may
you be comforted with His
perfect presence, and may you
be delivered quickly from
your feelings of anxiety.

Praise

LOVING FATHER, I PRAISE
You for Your deliverance. I
thank You for the ways You
gently care for me when I am
at my weakest, and how You
open up Your arms to care for
me in the most loving ways.

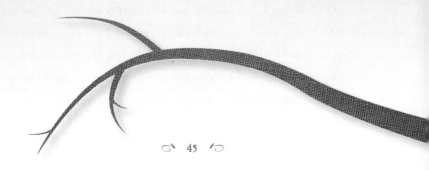

God's Peace for When You Are Filled with Fear

*F*ear. It wakes you, startled, from a deep sleep. It keeps you up at night. It dwells in the dusty shadows of the morning. It can haunt your dreams and push away any promises of a long night of peaceful sleep. Fear is real and powerful. If your mind is racing like a runaway freight train, full of fear, know this: our God is bigger than fear itself.

Jesus knows that fear is real, present even in the lives of His disciples. Remember when they were on the boat with Jesus and, while He was sleeping, a huge storm caused waves to crash over the sides of the boat (Mark 4:39–40)? The disciples cried out for Jesus to save them—and, as anyone would be, they were terrified. But Jesus' reply was straightforward. He didn't tell them it was all right to fear; instead, He said, "You of little faith, why are you so afraid?" He questioned their doubt and lack of faith in His ability to protect them.

Even though you cannot see Jesus now, know that He is with you. The Lord is right there beside you, as close as Jesus was to the disciples when He rebuked the wind and the waves. He brought calm to the storm. He calmed the disciples' fears. And He can calm your fears as well.

In His perfect and infallible Word, God repeatedly tells us not to fear. And why does He do this? He says not to fear because He is our mighty God and He promises to help us when we are afraid. The Creator of the universe, who hung the stars and fashioned the sun and molded man out of dust—He is with you now. He is Emmanuel, which is literally translated as "God with us." No matter what we face, we have the Lord on our side—and He is stronger than anything we are afraid of; in fact, He has overcome fear itself (1 John 4:18).

If you are still feeling fear, dear one, cry out to the Lord. Kneel at the side of your bed and ask Him to replace it with His perfect love. He is quick to answer His children as He surrounds us with His love. He will uphold you in your times of fear—and He has the power to cast out all fear in you, in me, and in all His children. What a promise!

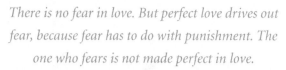

*There is no fear in love. But perfect love drives out
fear, because fear has to do with punishment. The
one who fears is not made perfect in love.*

1 JOHN 4:18

*I prayed to the LORD, and he answered me.
He freed me from all my fears.
Those who look to him for help will be radiant with joy;
no shadow of shame will darken their faces.
In my desperation I prayed, and the LORD listened;
he saved me from all my troubles.
For the angel of the LORD is a guard;
he surrounds and defends all who fear him.*

PSALM 34:4–7 NLT

*"Do not fear, for I am with you;
do not be dismayed, for I am your God.
I will strengthen you and help you;
I will uphold you with my righteous right hand."*

ISAIAH 41:10

*He got up, rebuked the wind and said to the waves,
"Quiet! Be still!" Then the wind died down and it
was completely calm. He said to his disciples, "Why
are you so afraid? Do you still have no faith?"*

MARK 4:39–40

Prayer

LORD, I AM SO AFRAID right now. I'm not able to close my eyes and sleep because I feel so fearful. You tell me to come to You with any request, and I'm asking You to abide with me right now. Please take away the fear that has its grip on me and fill me instead with the peace that comes with Your presence.

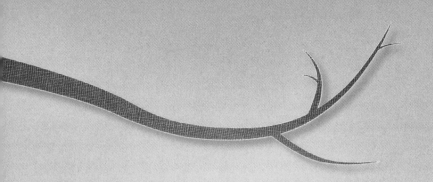

Blessing

MAY YOU FEEL GOD'S

presence all around you tonight.
Be comforted in the midst of
distress, and rest knowing that
He is with you. Because of
His great love for you, there is
no need to fear. May you find
courage and rest in knowing
He will cast out your fear.

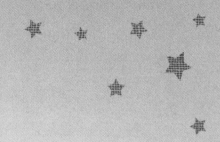

Praise

LORD, I PRAISE YOU FOR

Your peace in the midst of my
fear, for Your comfort in the
midst of my anxiety, and for
Your presence when I feel alone.

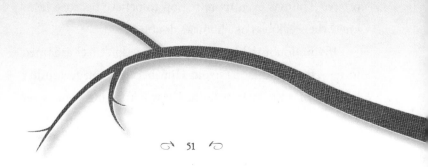

God's Peace for When You Are Filled with Doubt

This evening, when you climbed in bed and your mind was full of doubts, how did you feel? Were you berating yourself for doubting the goodness of God? Were you frustrated that your intellectual knowledge didn't seem to connect with your heart? Did you feel ashamed of your doubt?

Be comforted, dear friend. God is kind to those who doubt. Think of the disciple Thomas when he saw Jesus alive after Jesus was crucified. He doubted; in fact, to many Christians, he's known as "Doubting Thomas." However, when you look closely at God's Word, you realize that Jesus was not critical of Thomas's doubt. He didn't judge him or scoff at Thomas's unbelief. Instead, He gently held out His hands and spoke to Thomas saying, "Put your finger here, and see my hands; and put out your hand, and place it in my side. Do not disbelieve, but believe" (John 20:27 ESV). He offered Thomas even more reason to believe because Jesus knew the weakness of Thomas's doubt.

If you doubt the Lord in some way, don't feel ashamed to tell Him that. Don't avoid Him because you feel guilty because of your lack of faith. He won't shame you, sweet

child of His. He will help quell your doubts and your fears in just the ways you need. You only need to ask. He may not be with you physically on earth, but He can still make known His undeniable presence. Plead with the Lord to incline your heart to His testimonies; ask Him to remove the doubt you're feeling and replace it with a faith that could move mountains.

You may feel turmoil in your soul, causing you to toss around with feelings of unrest as you try to fall asleep. Ask the Lord to abide with you in it. As surely as the stars twinkle above and the moon shines a brilliant sheen on your quiet home, the Lord sees your doubt and loves you. He is faithful to hear your prayers.

Find rest for your soul tonight. Even though you doubt, you are still accepted by God and loved unconditionally.

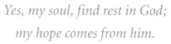

Yes, my soul, find rest in God;
my hope comes from him.

PSALM 62:5

Then he said to Thomas, "Put your finger here, and
see my hands; and put out your hand, and place
it in my side. Do not disbelieve, but believe.

JOHN 20:27 ESV

Only it must be in faith that he asks with no wavering
(no hesitating, no doubting). For the one who wavers
(hesitates, doubts) is like the billowing surge out at sea
that is blown hither and thither and tossed by the wind.

JAMES 1:6 AMP

Instantly Jesus reached out His hand and caught and held
him, saying to him, O you of little faith, why did you doubt?

MATTHEW 14:31 AMP

Jesus said to him, "If you can believe, all things are possible to
him who believes." Immediately the father of the child cried
out and said with tears, "Lord, I believe; help my unbelief!"

MARK 9:23–24 NKJV

Prayer

FATHER, YOU TELL ME TO come to You with anything, and tonight my heart feels full of doubt. Just as someone came to Jesus with his sick son and requested, "Help my unbelief," I ask for Your help this evening.

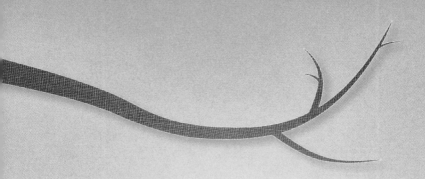

Blessing

WHEN YOU FEEL DOUBTS
mounting up, may you run
straight to the arms of Jesus.
May you be forthright with
your questions and confessions
and, even tonight, find comfort
in God's patience, tender
care, and gentle mercy.

Praise

I AM SO GRATEFUL TO

serve a God who is gentle
with my doubts. I praise You,
Father, for holding me closely
and tenderly, even when I
question You. I rejoice knowing
my Savior accepts me in all
my fallenness. Thank You
for never giving up on me!

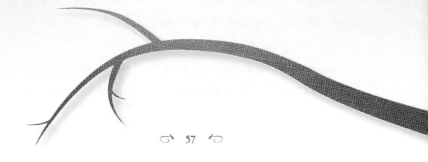

✳ God's Peace for When You Are Too Busy

*Y*ou can feel time ticking by, but sleep just will not come. As you toss and turn, pull the covers up and push them off, and stare at the rising numbers on the clock, you feel that familiar dread wash over you. If you don't fall asleep soon, tomorrow will be filled with exhaustion. You will meet your alarm with dread and fatigue, but try as you might, you simply cannot fall into a deep sleep. Instead, the endless list of what needs to get done fills your mind, pumping your body with adrenaline at an hour your body is supposed to be relaxing.

Busyness is sometimes a necessity and can even be a blessing for a season, but when it's keeping you up at night, something needs to change. My friend, whatever you are overwhelmed by this evening—the list of things running through your head that needs to be completed, the errands that need to be run, the deadlines that need to be met, the stacks of bills that need to be paid—remember this: you can rest tonight. Your biggest priority right now is sleep; everything else is secondary. We can only live well when we are getting enough rest.

Rejoice in the knowledge that the Lord desires rest for you too; after all, He is the One who created a day of rest

while creating the world. He was busy filling the newly-created oceans with fish and setting the sun in the sky and breathing life into man's lungs, but after He was finished, He rested. He didn't worry about creating more new animals or adding one more new species of bird—instead, He took time to stop. He saw that what He did was good. He was satisfied with His work, and He wanted to rest. He wants his people to live rest-filled lives too. He even commands us to rest in (Exodus 20:8–11).

Our lives can get crammed with work obligations, raising a family, cultivating relationships, and other good things, but within the rush of busyness we need the rhythm and settledness of a Sabbath. Consider ways you can cut your to-do list. Try to say no more often. Rearrange your list of priorities. Instead of working against the way you were created, embrace the benefits of rest—both physical and spiritual. The Lord is ready to help you and desires all good things for you—look to Him, the calm in the eye of the storm. His peace can quiet every bit of chaos in your life, beloved. Cease your striving and be still.

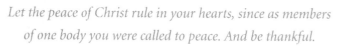

Let the peace of Christ rule in your hearts, since as members of one body you were called to peace. And be thankful.

COLOSSIANS 3:15

"Remember the Sabbath day by keeping it holy. Six days you shall labor and do all your work, but the seventh day is a sabbath to the Lord your God. On it you shall not do any work, neither you, nor your son or daughter, nor your male or female servant, nor your animals, nor any foreigner residing in your towns. For in six days the Lord made the heavens and the earth, the sea, and all that is in them, but he rested on the seventh day. Therefore the Lord blessed the Sabbath day and made it holy."

EXODUS 20:8–11

May the Lord of peace himself give you peace at all times and in every way. The Lord be with all of you.

2 THESSALONIANS 3:16

*"Be still, and know that I am God.
I will be exalted among the nations,
I will be exalted in the earth."*

PSALM 46:10

Prayer

BUSYNESS SEEMS TO BE the anthem of my life lately, Lord. It's loud and overwhelming and much too chaotic. You tell me to be still and trust in You, and it's so hard for me to do that. Give me wisdom for reprioritizing my schedule and strength to rest in Your care.

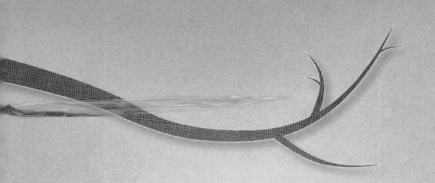

Blessing

MAY YOU COLLAPSE IN
the arms of the One holding
everything together; He
is to be trusted. Even
now, in the dark hours of
this night, may you begin
feeling God's peace working
through your busy mind,
quieting you with His love.

Praise

YOU CAME SO THAT WE
may have peace, Jesus. Thank
You for sacrificing Yourself
for the good of mankind so
Your peace can reign in my
heart. Your humility and
self-sacrificial love is to be
praised forever and ever!

God's Peace for When You Are Discontent

*D*iscontentment lies in so many areas of our lives: money, possessions, life stage, appearance, career, and more, and it's hard to find sleep when it's your struggle. It's a tool of the devil. It leads to dissatisfaction with God and His provision rather than being thankful for what He's given. It opens up the temptation to take provisions into your own hands and, if you aren't careful, it will choke you spiritually and emotionally, affecting you in very negative ways. Are you feeling this urge right now, dear one?

If so, you are not alone—feeling discontent is a common struggle for all of humanity. This world is a restless world, constantly telling us to strive for more, better, higher. In this broken existence, our hearts are always searching for that one more thing that eludes us, the one thing that will make us happy and satisfied. But, here's the important thing to remember: the Lord calls us away from a life of discontentment. He doesn't want to see our hearts searching the world for something else to fill us up. Instead, *He* wants to fill us up—to help us be content in all circumstances, not just when we finally get a promotion or at last become parents or save up enough money for those shoes.

What area of your life are you currently feeling unyielding discontentment? Tell the Lord your struggles; He longs to hear them. In the Bible, Paul gives great insight into contentment. He says that he has learned to be content in whatever circumstance he's in—whether having abundance or suffering, whether being filled or going hungry, he knew this truth: only the Lord can satisfy us (Philippians 4:12). It is He who fills us. It is He who satisfies us. When we feel discontent, we seek to fill a void that is reserved only for God. Instead of rushing to fill it with one more thing, beloved, call to Him to fill that void with His fullness of peace.

As you lay your head back down, sleep deeply knowing the Lord knows your needs. He knows your heart. He knows your life's circumstances. And He is more than able to give abundantly—in His will, in His timing, and in His perfect plan. Rest in that knowledge tonight. You have everything you need.

*I am not saying this because I am in need, for I have learned
to be content whatever the circumstances. I know what it is
to be in need, and I know what it is to have plenty. I have
learned the secret of being content in any and every situation,
whether well fed or hungry, whether living in plenty or in
want. I can do all this through him who gives me strength.*

PHILIPPIANS 4:11–13

*But godliness with contentment is great gain. For we brought
nothing into the world, and we can take nothing out of it.
But if we have food and clothing, we will be content with
that. Those who want to get rich fall into temptation and a
trap and into many foolish and harmful desires that plunge
people into ruin and destruction. For the love of money is
a root of all kinds of evil. Some people, eager for money,
have wandered from the faith and pierced themselves with
many griefs. But you, man of God, flee from all this, and
pursue righteousness, godliness, faith, love, endurance and
gentleness. Fight the good fight of the faith. Take hold of
the eternal life to which you were called when you made
your good confession in the presence of many witnesses.*

1 TIMOTHY 6:6–12

*The fear of the LORD leads to life;
then one rests content, untouched by trouble.*

PROVERBS 19:23

Prayer

IT IS SO HARD FOR ME TO be content this evening, Lord. I am wrestling with this discontentment, but it feels like a stronghold, and I don't know if I have enough strength to overcome it. Please fill me with Your Spirit and satisfy my void in a way that only You can.

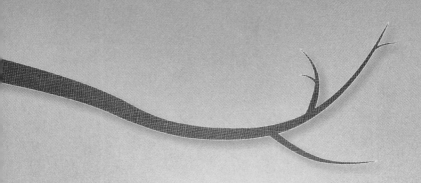

Blessing

MAY YOUR EYES BE SO
fixed on the heavenly prize,
Jesus Christ, that everything
else falls to the wayside.
For all earthly things are
inferior to the gift we have in
Jesus. May you revel in that
knowledge and feel completely
filled up by His provision.

Praise

WHEN I FEEL MOST
satisfied, I am resting in
You, Lord. I rejoice in Your
salvation; discontentment
doesn't need to govern me,
and You are quick to save me
from this striving for more.
Thank You for Your never-
ending love and mercy.

God's Peace for When You Feel Unforgiving

Tonight even your cozy bed can't swallow up the feelings vying for your attention. They're strong feelings, powerful and passionate. To sum it up, you're harboring unforgiveness toward someone, and it feels good to let your anger simmer over time, stewing in your frustration and putting the lid on any grace.

Friend, we have all been there. We have all lain awake in the night, too riled up to hear the Lord's call to forgiveness and rest. Forgiving does not come naturally in this fallen world. It feels easier and better to resent someone than love them, especially if they have wronged us to a degree that cuts deep in our heart, never to be forgotten. But, be warned— every simmering pot of unforgiveness eventually boils over, and the poison seeps into your life, affecting your body and spirit, your family and relationships, your moods and emotions, and even your health.

Be assured that when refusing to forgive someone, it's not affecting him or her—it's affecting *you*. Even now you're losing precious sleep. Instead of greeting the morning feeling refreshed and renewed, you'll face the day tired, exhausted, and bitter. It's not worth it, beloved. Grace shown to others

is difficult to grasp because it doesn't feel fair. We are a society that wants everything to be fair. We want equality. And we don't want to be wronged. Often, forgiveness requires us to be humble enough to step back from the world's ways and submit to God's ways.

Although forgiveness is difficult, it's truly worth extending. Forgiveness equals freedom. Unforgiveness equals bondage. Be freed tonight. You are precious in the sight of the Lord, and He longs for nothing more than to see the bondage of unforgiveness fall off your shoulders. Utter a small prayer of forgiveness, even if it's just asking the Lord for strength to forgive. That's a step. It's a step toward wholeness, a step toward the Lord, and a huge leap in the direction God wants you to go. Just as unforgiveness can keep you up at night, forgiveness can bring a peace that helps you sleep deeply, gladly, soundly. Do you want that type of rest? Go to the Lord who readily forgives our sins. He will help you. He offers healing in the wounds we think are too deep to touch, too painful to heal.

Start on the path of forgiveness tonight, beloved—you will begin to feel transformed in the best possible way. Be brave, be bold, and see beauty unfold in your life.

*Bear with each other and forgive one
another if any of you has a grievance against
someone. Forgive as the Lord forgave you.*
COLOSSIANS 3:13

*Then Peter came to Jesus and asked, "Lord, how many
times shall I forgive my brother or sister who sins
against me? Up to seven times?" Jesus answered, "I
tell you, not seven times, but seventy-seven times."*
MATTHEW 18:21–22

*For he has rescued us from the dominion of darkness
and brought us into the kingdom of the Son he loves, in
whom we have redemption, the forgiveness of sins.*
COLOSSIANS 1:13–14

Prayer

HEAVENLY FATHER, IT IS so hard for me to forgive others. Right now, I feel so much frustration and resentment in my heart and it's hard for me to fall asleep. Please remind me of Your own forgiveness toward me and how You paid the ultimate atonement for my sins—through Your very own Son. Walk with me along the path of forgiveness and give me strength in each step.

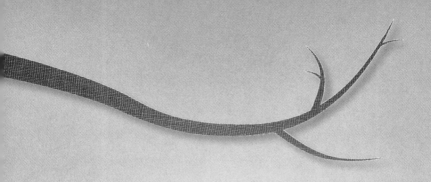

Blessing

MAY EACH STEP TOWARD
forgiveness bring you closer to
freedom. May the Lord bring
renewal to your mind and
heart as you submit to His
ways and His will, and may
you find liberty and great joy
in practicing forgiveness daily.

Praise

I PRAISE YOU, FATHER,

for the forgiveness You show

to me each and every day.

Thank You for the strength

You give in helping me forgive

others who have wronged me.

God's Peace for When You Are Exhausted

*E*xhaustion is a strange thing. Sometimes when we are exhausted, the very thing we need—sleep— won't come easily. Exhaustion comes in many different forms and can creep up on you in a hurry until you're left feeling utterly worn out. Are you emotionally exhausted? Perhaps you just experienced an ongoing, devastating loss that has left your heart in shreds, too tired to even cry. Maybe you've given everything you have to a relationship, and while it's repaired in a fragile state, you simply have nothing more to give. Or maybe you're physically exhausted. Are you up with a newborn at all hours of the night, willing this child to go to sleep? Or are you trying to recover from an injury, and physical therapy requires every single ounce of your strength? Or, is the process of aging just crippling you in small ways that add up to a mountain of exhaustion?

If you're watching the night hours tick on by, exhausted and yet not sleeping, try not to fret. The Lord knows what you need. He knows how tired you are, how you're craving sleep in the deepest way, and He is ready to help. Here is some encouragement for you, tired traveler.

The Bible addresses exhaustion and weariness in a poignant way. It constantly points to a God who never tires,

never sleeps, and never gives up on us. In fact, Isaiah proclaims God's strength, and he begins Isaiah 40:28–29 (ESV) with a proclamation: "Have you not known? Have you not heard? The LORD . . . does not faint or grow weary . . . He gives power to the faint." What a promise you can cling to during this time of exhaustion! If you're worried that one night of rest won't be enough for your exhausted self, claim the strength that is yours through God's Word. It is infiltrated with His promise to give strength to the weary, and that includes you.

Remember, God doesn't call us to be exhausted; He wants us to be whole. He wants us to be free from the weight this world can bring. He wants our hearts to be glad and joy-filled. That's why He sent His Son Jesus into this broken world—to restore our connection with God so that we can bask in the true and lasting healing, restoration, and rejuvenation only He can give. Take heart, friend. It's not entirely up to you to find rest for your soul; all you need to do is raise your tired head to the Lord.

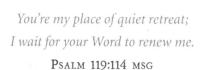

You're my place of quiet retreat;
I wait for your Word to renew me.

PSALM 119:114 MSG

Return to your rest, my soul,
for the LORD has been good to you.

PSALM 116:7

But I have calmed and quieted myself,
I am like a weaned child with its mother;
like a weaned child I am content.

PSALM 131:2

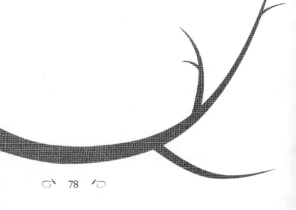

Prayer

PRECIOUS SAVIOR, I AM SO
tired tonight, yet am not able
to fall into a deep, untroubled
sleep. Instead of focusing on my
own struggles and exhaustion,
help me turn my eyes to You,
God of the weary. I know You
love to help Your children, and
I ask that You would help me
sleep soundly tonight, comforted
with Your loving presence.

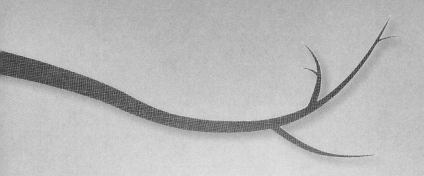

Blessing

WEARY TRAVELER, MAY
you rest your head on the
shoulder of the Lord tonight.
May you wake feeling refreshed
in every sense, full of peace
and hope and joy for a new
morning and expectation of the
Lord's provision and strength.

Praise

DEAREST FATHER,
thank You for Your holy
and God-breathed Scripture.
Thank You for the promises
throughout Your Word; they
sustain me at my weakest
and fill me with hope for the
future and for tomorrow.

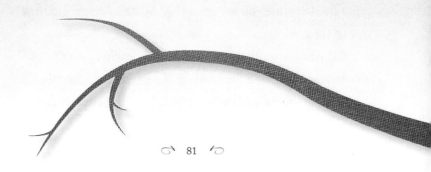

God's Peace for When You Are Waiting

*I*n life, it seems like we are always waiting for something. Waiting for the weekend, waiting to graduate from school, waiting to find that special someone, waiting for that job callback. Waiting can often feel like biding our time, and many times waiting lends itself to feelings of impatience. Even now, as you're trying to fall asleep, you probably feel impatient—not just for sleep to come, but also because you're tired of waiting.

What are you waiting for? Tonight, it might be something exciting, like welcoming a new baby into your family. Or it could be something somber, such as waiting for test results to come back. Whether you are waiting on something joyful or potentially challenging, it's causing you to miss out on some much-needed rest.

When you are feeling impatient, sometimes the best thing to do is focus on something else—and for believers, it can be helpful to focus your attention heavenward. Why not use the time you are spending awake by spending time with the Lord?

If you are waiting for an upcoming exciting event, concentrate on praising the Lord for His goodness. After all, He is the One who helped orchestrate these joyful circumstances

in your life. If you're waiting for your upcoming wedding day, thank Him for your loving future spouse. If you're anticipating a vacation, thank God for providing the means to break away from routines and for having time to play.

On the other hand, if you are impatiently waiting for something such as test results or a child you dream of yet don't have, or if you simply wish for a friend in this season of loneliness, think upon the Lord. Consider ways He has shown His faithfulness in your life, and remind yourself of His goodness to come. In this waiting period, it may feel as if God's promises are true for everyone's life but your own, or that the waiting might continue indefinitely. Let me tell you this: there is a season for everything. And while you are in this waiting season, the best thing to do is reflect on God's goodness and praise Him for it.

Settle back in your bed, fluff the pillow one more time, and remind yourself that the Lord is the same yesterday, today, and tomorrow. He will never leave you or forsake you. And as you wait, He is busy orchestrating the perfect plan for your life.

I would have lost heart, unless I had believed
That I would see the goodness of the LORD
In the land of the living.
Wait on the LORD;
Be of good courage,
And He shall strengthen your heart;
Wait, I say, on the LORD!

PSALM 27:13–14 NKJV

We wait in hope for the LORD;
he is our help and our shield.
In him our hearts rejoice,
for we trust in his holy name.
May your unfailing love be with us, LORD,
even as we put our hope in you.

PSALM 33:20–22

The Lord is good to those who wait for him,
to the soul who seeks him.

LAMENTATIONS 3:25 ESV

Prayer

IT IS SO HARD TO WAIT, Lord. Sometimes waiting takes a big toll on me, and in the midst of waiting and yearning, I forget to praise You. Help me to always remember You, whether I'm waiting for something good or something potentially painful. Teach me patience and the gift of resting in Your goodness as I fix my eyes on You.

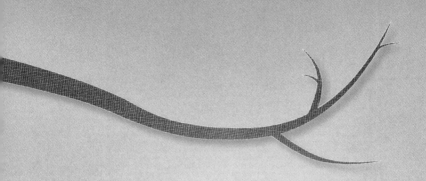

Blessing

IN THIS WAITING TIME,
may you grow ever closer
to the Lord. May your
mouth be filled with praises
toward the Most High King,
and may you look at these
days of waiting as sweet
communion with the Lord.

Praise

THANK YOU FOR YOUR
goodness, Lord. You are
faithful to your children in
every season—whether it's
full of waiting, joy, sadness, or
loss—You are there with us.
I praise You, Father, for Your
constant presence in my life.

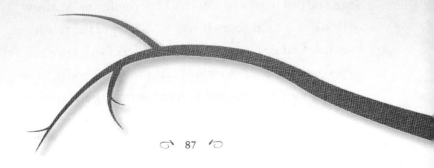

God's Peace for When You Are Filled with Grief

There are many things that can keep you awake during the night, but one of the hardest to overcome is a grief-filled heart. Are you grieving this evening? Be comforted, dear friend. Find solace in the ever-compassionate, always present God.

You may feel lonely, angry, and hopeless. You may be filled with an utter sense of loss. You may feel betrayed, tired, and full of doubt. In grief, you can experience so many feelings—and other times you can simply feel very tired and want to dull your emotions, stuff your grief down into the crevices of your heart, and keep moving ahead. Grief can resurface for no rhyme or reason. It can overtake you at the most peculiar of times, and on this side of heaven, it can be so difficult to accept the fact that grief is a reality for everyone; it's an unavoidable part of life.

Dear friend, resist the urge to push your grief down. Jesus said that those who mourn will be comforted (Matthew 5:4). It's okay to let yourself grieve. It's okay to feel an emotion that God gave you. When you feel grief well up, it's an opportunity to pour out your heart to God. If you're lying in bed, your pillow covered in tears, or tossing and turning

with the numbness of being worn out from grief, cry out to the Lord. He loves you and wants you to run to Him. Even if your words come in fits and bursts and you don't feel you're making any sense, know that the Lord understands perfectly what you're trying to say. He knows what's in your heart—the Holy Spirit is interceding for you, even if all you can do is cry.

Give yourself permission to mourn, feel sad, feel angry, reflect on memories, and everything in between. God knows what you're thinking and feeling already, but the very act of releasing your pain to Him sets you up to receive His grace and mercy as never before. Try to focus on pouring your heart out to the Lord, or, if it's all you can do, simply sit in his presence. Read through the Psalms to give voice to the emotions you feel. Reading Scripture, particularly Psalms, is very comforting for the soul—the power of God's Word gives voice to the emotions you feel and supernatural strength toward healing.

At last, when your eyes grow tired and you begin falling asleep, ask the Lord to bind up your broken heart. Ask Him to renew your spirit while you sleep. Rest, beloved; the Lord is holding you.

*Praise be to the God and Father of our Lord Jesus Christ,
the Father of compassion and the God of all comfort, who
comforts us in all our troubles, so that we can comfort those in
any trouble with the comfort we ourselves receive from God.*

2 Corinthians 1:3–4

*The Lord is close to the brokenhearted
and saves those who are crushed in spirit.*

Psalm 34:18

*When Jesus saw her weeping . . . he was deeply moved in his
spirit and greatly troubled. And he said, "Where have you laid
him?" They said to him, "Lord, come and see." Jesus wept.*

John 11:33–35 esv

Prayer

OH FATHER, I NEED YOU. I am deeply troubled and broken-hearted. My heart is aching with sadness, and I desperately need You to comfort me in all my sorrow.

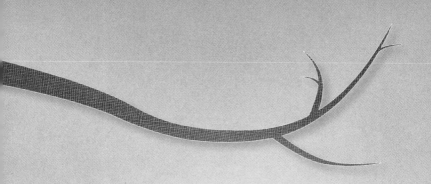

Blessing

MAY THE TENDER CARE

of the Father rest upon you
tonight. May your sorrow and
grief be lifted as steadily as the
sun rises and the stars begin to
dim as the Lord cares for you.

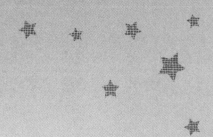

Praise

I PRAISE YOU, HEAVENLY

Father, for the tender mercy
You give each of Your
children, and in this hour,
especially me. I am needy
and in need of a Savior; You
are the rescuer of my soul.

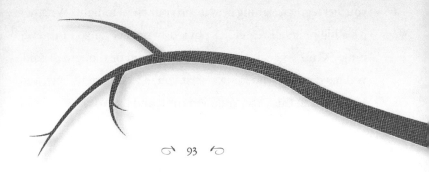

God's Peace for When You Are Filled with Regret

*Y*ou've been lying in bed for hours now, but sleep just won't come. Every time you close your eyes or try to relax, it feels hopeless. Instead of looking forward to a good night of rest and a new day tomorrow, you can't shake the feeling—the feeling of regret.

It could be regret of how you spent your time today or treated your children or spouse. Maybe you're filled with regret over what you ate, the gossip you helped spread in the break room, or the frustration that filled your tone when talking to your mom on the phone. Or perhaps it's deeper than that: you feel regret over something that happened last month, last year, or even a decade ago. Angry words that bubbled up and broke a friendship, the addiction that trapped you and left you picking up the pieces of a broken life, the mistake that cost you more than you ever imagined. Everyone has regrets, some bigger than others, and they have the power to keep us up in all hours of the night for a lifetime.

Dear sister or brother, is this ringing true in your life? Do you feel regret weighing heavily on your chest tonight? Whether it's a big or small regret, it's obviously impacting you this evening. While you can't change what you did or thought or said, you have a God who knows what you're feeling right now, and He speaks to this exact situation through His Word.

Christ tells us to forgive and ask for forgiveness—and if you haven't done it already, it's time to take that first step. Come before your heavenly Father and ask Him for help. You'll be amazed at the weight that's lifted off your shoulders. The Bible also tells us that when we ask for forgiveness, the Lord forgets our transgressions—what an incredible gift! If you are filled with regret tonight, focus on God's gift of forgiveness. Whether you need to ask the Lord for forgiveness, call up an old friend, or even forgive yourself, it's the genesis of being free from regret.

Scripture is also so comforting in times when we feel regret. There are countless verses that assure us of complete forgiveness and redemption. If you are a new creation in Christ, you have been redeemed, cleansed, and restored. You no longer wear filthy rags, but a robe of righteousness. Embrace that joy, dear friend. Rejoice in the Lord's goodness toward all of us—for we are all sinners who have failed, but Christ's blood redeems us once and for all. Meditate on Scripture right now. Ask the Lord to open your eyes to His truths and righteousness. Be filled with hope, for you no longer need to be burdened by regret; you have been restored.

*Brothers and sisters, I do not consider myself yet to
have taken hold of it. But one thing I do: Forgetting
what is behind and straining toward what is ahead,
I press on toward the goal to win the prize for which
God has called me heavenward in Christ Jesus.*

PHILIPPIANS 3:13–14

*If we confess our sins, he is faithful and will forgive us
our sins and purify us from all unrighteousness.*

1 JOHN 1:9

*Let me hear joy and gladness;
let the bones that you have broken rejoice.
Hide your face from my sins,
and blot out all my iniquities.*

PSALM 51:8–9 ESV

Prayer

LORD, YOU KNOW HOW much regret I am feeling right now. But I know Your Word is true, and You promise to forget my sins if I ask for Your forgiveness. Help me believe those words, and please remove this burden from my heart so I can fully rejoice in Your cleansing and healing.

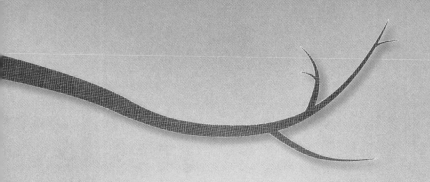

Blessing

MAY YOU EXPERIENCE
the everlasting forgiveness of
the Father, reveling in the
freedom that comes when we
confess our sins to Him. May
you fully know how forgiven
and free you truly are.

Praise

I PRAISE YOU, MY
Almighty and all-merciful God,
for Your grace. I thank You for
Your kindness toward me; even
when I make big mistakes,
regret doesn't have to be my
lifelong companion. Thank You
for always forgiving me and
carrying my burdens for me.

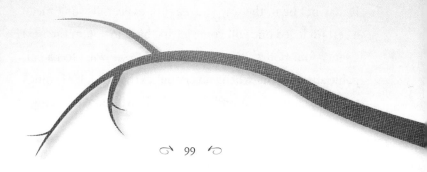

God's Peace for When You Are Missing a Loved One

*M*issing a loved one is a very lonely feeling. The only thing to really resolve the ache of loneliness is to actually see the person you're missing. But many times, it's not that easy. You may miss your mother who passed away last year, your daughter studying abroad, or your husband on a long business trip. Even though it may not be an easily fixable situation, there is a longing in your heart that cannot be denied.

It's a mixture of sadness, grief, discontentment, loneliness, and maybe even a bit of anxiety when you're missing someone you love. When you miss someone, that void can't truly be filled unless they are in your arms, hugging you. But that doesn't answer the question of how you can get to sleep tonight, when you're feeling their absence so tangibly.

The answer is simple, but it's not simplistic. Call to God to fill your void. He hears you, and He will come to your aid. It may not be in the way you want or expect. It won't mean a certain loved one will come jetting back to you in the next twenty-four hours. It doesn't mean that you won't feel a palpable absence. But when you cry out to the Lord, He is quick to bring compassion and comfort. He will be your refuge,

dear friend. He will console you in His perfect, timely, all-knowing way.

We can find comfort in the presence of our God—especially when we are troubled or missing a loved one. In the Bible, 2 Corinthians 1:4 (NKJV) says that the God of all comfort "comforts us in all our tribulation." Cling to that truth, dear sister or brother. Look for the Lord's presence this evening. He can fill that empty, cavernous hole that feels so desperate. Pour out your heart to the Lord; He will sustain you in your most pain-filled moments. He will provide a light in the darkness; He is a reprieve in the pain, a provider to the weary, and a strength to the weak.

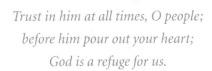

Trust in him at all times, O people;
before him pour out your heart;
God is a refuge for us.

PSALM 62:8 ESV

He will answer the prayers of the needy;
he will not reject their prayers.

PSALM 102:17 NCV

For the Lamb in the midst of the throne will be their
shepherd, and he will guide them to springs of living water,
and God will wipe away every tear from their eyes.

REVELATION 7:17 ESV

Prayer

DEAR FATHER, I MISS
_____ so much
right now. The ache I feel is
almost unbearable and the void
is so palpable. I know You will
sustain me, and I ask You to
come quickly to my aid, Lord
Jesus. Ease the pain I feel in
my heart and wipe away my
tears with Your loving hand.

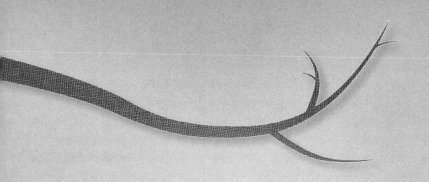

Blessing

DEAR CHILD OF GOD,
may you be utterly comforted
by the One who knows you
intimately. May you find
a reprieve from the pain
through the tender mercy
of the Lord who hears every
cry and sees every tear.

Praise

YOU ARE A GOOD,
loving, compassionate God
and I praise You for Your
loving kindness toward me.
The grief I feel right now is
tangible, but I am grateful
for Your presence, which is
also so apparent to me when
I'm struggling. Thank You,
Lord, for Your comfort.

God's Peace for When You Are Suffering

The heart of the Christian story revolves around suffering. Jesus suffered on the cross for our sin, providing a way of redemption for us sinners. Suffering is something none of us want to go through, yet we are all prone to at some time in our lives. Are you walking a difficult path through suffering right now? At times it may seem like there's no end in sight, but don't lose hope—for there is an end, there is always an end if you're a believer. If you're having trouble sleeping because of your current state of suffering, be it physical, emotional, or spiritual, be reminded of God's holy Word and the messages of hope within.

While the heart of the Christian faith is about suffering, it also is about redemption. God takes broken things and makes them beautiful. He is the Creator of redemption. As you lie in bed wrestling with your suffering, it can be so hard—and seem almost cruel—to be told that your suffering will birth something beautiful. Yet the Lord speaks truth in His Word: although those who love Him often go through suffering, it can be a time to draw ever so close to the heart of the Lord. During times of suffering, death, pain, and darkness are turned to rebirth, healing, and light when you are part of the Christian story.

As Christians, we are to expect suffering. In John 16:33, Jesus said, "In this world you will have trouble," but He followed up that statement with a beautiful, hope-filled statement: "Take heart." You may wonder, *Why? Why should I take heart when my suffering is so acute?* The answer is this: Jesus has overcome the world through the death He suffered on the cross. Because of His work on the cross, you can have hope in your suffering. The Lord has overcome evil, and He will bring you to a place of splendor.

Tonight, even in the middle of your suffering, take comfort in the words of the Lord, our Savior. Know that your suffering will be painful, but the Lord's ability to strengthen you during this time—even grieve with you in your pain—can help bandage up even the most broken of hearts. Your present suffering, dear sister or brother, will reveal a greater glory. Fall asleep feeling confident of the Lord's plan for your life; He will use suffering for good—He promises.

I consider that our present sufferings are not worth comparing with the glory that will be revealed in us.

ROMANS 8:18

And the God of all grace, who called you to his eternal glory in Christ, after you have suffered a little while, will himself restore you and make you strong, firm and steadfast.

1 PETER 5:10

"I have told you these things, so that in me you may have peace. In this world you will have trouble. But take heart! I have overcome the world."

JOHN 16:33

Prayer

FATHER GOD, BE NEAR ME in my suffering tonight. It is sometimes hard for me to accept that suffering is a part of life, but it is comforting to know that You are with me always and are working all things together for good. Renew my tired spirit and continually put before me the hope each new day brings.

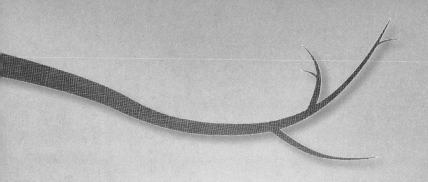

Blessing

MAY YOU EXPERIENCE HOW
deep and rich and wide the
love of God can be in your
life. May you see your present
sufferings as nothing compared
to the future glory that will be
revealed in heaven. In the midst
of your suffering, may you reach
for God's hand and cling to the
redemptive work of the Father.

Praise

THANK YOU, ABBA, FOR YOUR
perfect work. You take the ugly,
painful suffering in this world and
somehow turn it into beauty. You
took the dust of the earth and
fashioned it into human beings.
You made the glorious, green earth
out of nothing. And You will take
my own personal struggles and
make them into precious gems.

God's Peace for When You Feel Betrayed

*B*etrayal hurts. It cuts like a knife into the most vulnerable parts of our hearts and leaves us feeling used and worn out, utterly alone. Whether a friend or family member has betrayed you, it hurts—a lot. It feels like the pain will never subside, and whenever that person's name comes up, the knife twists, bringing to mind the same scalding feelings of betrayal, the same throb of pain in your heart.

My friend, are you are feeling alone and afraid tonight because of a betrayal new or old? Are those feelings of shock, dismay, and brokenness bubbling their way to the surface once again? You may feel as though you want to give up, and you might want to see your betrayer hurting as much as you. But, let me tell you the truth: revenge will only bring more pain, more heartbreak, and deeper grief.

Instead of inflicting more grief upon your life, cling to Jesus, the One who will never betray you. Run to the One who never sinned, yet was betrayed by one of His close friends, leading to a painful death. He knows your pain. He knows exactly what you are going through right now. He has been there and has walked through the very feelings you are wrestling with. Go to the Lord with your unrest, and find

solace in His arms. Nothing—*nothing*—can separate You from His love.

God's Word can be a place of comfort for you this evening. The psalmist David knew what it felt like to be betrayed. This is someone God favored—yet David still felt the deep sting of disloyalty. He said, "Even my close friend in whom I trusted, who ate my bread, has lifted his heel against me" (Psalm 41:9 ESV). In our fallen world, we will be betrayed. But we can find solace in the Lord, for we worship a God who will never turn His back on us. We praise a Father who can only abide in purity and love.

Ask the almighty Healer to bind up your broken and angry heart tonight. Close your eyes and relax, knowing that He is your constant friend, an ever-present help in trouble. He will help you rise above your embarrassment and pain; He will give you the grace to find healing and beauty in the most difficult of circumstances. Nothing, beloved child of the Father, can separate you from His love.

He was oppressed and afflicted,
yet he did not open his mouth;
he was led like a lamb to the slaughter,
and as a sheep before its shearers is silent,
so he did not open his mouth.

ISAIAH 53:7

For I am convinced that neither death nor life, neither
angels nor demons, neither the present nor the future,
nor any powers, neither height nor depth, nor anything
else in all creation, will be able to separate us from
the love of God that is in Christ Jesus our Lord.

ROMANS 8:38–39

It is better to take refuge in the LORD
than to trust in humans.

PSALM 118:8

Do not take revenge, my dear friends, but leave
room for God's wrath, for it is written: "It is
mine to avenge; I will repay," says the Lord.

ROMANS 12:19

Prayer

LORD, YOU KNOW EXACTLY what betrayal feels like, for You were betrayed by one of Your disciples. Right now I am feeling betrayed and alone. Come near to me, dear Lord, and grant me relief from this anguish. Remind me of Your steadfast faithfulness; I need to know You will never leave me.

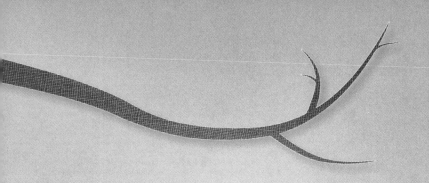

Blessing

MAY THE CONSTANCY OF
the Lord's presence give you
peace this evening, especially
when you are feeling distressed.
May you revel in His care and
find relief for your pained heart.

Praise

THANK YOU, FATHER GOD,
for the promises You speak in
Your Word. When I am alone,
You promise to be with me.
When I am afraid, You promise
to calm my fears. And when I
am feeling betrayed, You promise
to be my Comforter. I praise the
Lord, the keeper of my heart!

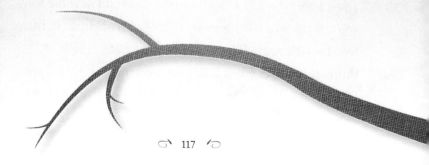

God's Peace for When You Feel Inundated by Life's Demands

od, I'm worn out, you pray as the hours tick by. You know your alarm is set to go off in just a few hours, but you haven't had any sleep. You feel too overwhelmed to relax your shoulders and breathe deeply. You may be facing a personal, heartbreaking crisis right now—and don't know how to deal with the pain. You may feel that at the end of each day you got nothing accomplished, even though you skipped lunch and didn't sit down until 10 p.m. Maybe you committed to something that you now realize was way too big for you to handle, and you feel frazzled and fearful.

Whatever the circumstance, you're now wrestling late into the night with the heavy burden of feeling inundated by life's demands. You're carrying more than you're able, but you fear if you let go, everything will come toppling down.

Fellow traveler, listen to the words of the psalmist in Psalm 142:3 (NLT). He said, "When I am overwhelmed, you alone know the way I should turn." Do you know the way you should turn when you are feeling overwhelmed in life? Don't search yourself for a hidden reserve of strength. Don't think, *If I just can give a little bit more tomorrow, I'll feel better.* No, dear friend. The answer is not in you; it's in the Lord.

Cry to Him—if you don't have it all figured out, it's okay. God doesn't ask us to be spic and span when we fall before His throne. In Psalm 61:2 (NKJV), the psalmist said he cries to the Lord when he is overwhelmed. "From the end of the earth I will cry to You, when my heart is overwhelmed; lead me to the rock that is higher than I." God can lead you to a higher place—out of the suffocating circumstances that are clamoring for your attention, your time, your energy, your heart. Not only can He lead you there, but He will carry your burden for you. No longer do you need to feel overloaded and overrun. Hand it over to God. Tell Him how exhausted you feel. He won't be disappointed in you.

Tonight, turn to Him. Run into the arms of your Father; He is full of mercy, love, and grace. Breathe deeply, child. The Lord is fighting for you. You don't need to stumble under the weight of exhaustion anymore. You can emerge, energized by the goodness of God.

Hear my prayer, LORD;
let my cry for help come to you.
Do not hide your face from me
when I am in distress.
Turn your ear to me;
when I call, answer me quickly.

PSALM 102:1–2

We are merely moving shadows, and all our busy
rushing ends in nothing. We heap up wealth, not
knowing who will spend it. And so, Lord, where
do I put my hope? My only hope is in you.

PSALM 39:6–7 NLT

Now to him who is able to do immeasurably more than all
we ask or imagine, according to his power that is at work
within us, to him be glory in the church and in Christ Jesus
throughout all generations, for ever and ever! Amen.

EPHESIANS 3:20–21

Prayer

FATHER GOD, YOU KNOW I am feeling utterly inundated and worn out by the demands in my life. You know that I am trying to do everything out of my own strength, trying to prove I can do it all. I can't. I run to You, in these late hours, to take refuge in Your arms— the only place of true rest.

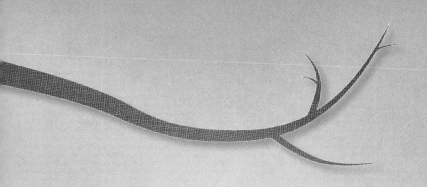

Blessing

MAY YOU FIND FREEDOM
from exhaustion and your
overwhelmed state of
mind, trusting the Lord is
strong enough to help you,
and in laying down your
idol of "doing," may you
contentedly walk with the
Lord beside cool waters and
lie down in green pastures.

Praise

I OFFER YOU MY MOST
sincere praise, Lord God. You
are able to free me from my
endless cycle of being too
busy, and instead help me
sing a new song: a praise of
deliverance and joy, for You
have saved my soul. You
have given me new life!

God's Peace for When You Feel Discouraged

hen evening falls and a hush comes over the night, you begin getting ready for bed. You wash your face, brush your teeth, and go through the nightly routine. But if you're burdened by a feeling of discouragement, falling asleep isn't an easy routine as on a normal night.

Discouragement may come from a battle you've been fighting for years—a tense family relationship, a physical ailment, a career path that doesn't seem to be panning out. Or your discouragement could lie in something more recent—a bad week at work, a disagreement with your sister, another negative pregnancy test, an overall feeling of failure. Oh dear one, we have all felt the discouragement you feel at one time or another. The question is, what are you going to do with it?

It's all too easy to wallow in discouragement and turn your face away from hope. But that result is simply not of the Lord. It's what the enemy wants—he wants us to look at our problem instead of the Savior. The enemy wants us to give up the good fight, and look downcast at the days ahead. He wants us to stumble and fall, shaking our head at the future, and he'll do anything to keep us in that state of

mind. But there is good news: Jesus has triumphed over the enemy. Through Him, we have everlasting hope and can live encouraged through all circumstances.

Whatever situation you are in right now, there is hope right where you are. There is always hope. The Bible clearly says in Romans 5:5 that hope does not disappoint us (NASB). God's love has been poured into our hearts, and because of that, our lives and whole eternal future have been changed. You may not feel a lot of hope in your heart right now. You may not see victory ahead, and you may not be sure what you can do to change things. But you don't have to have things all figured out at this moment; just collapse on the One who is weaving a unique story in your life. He will use the discouragement you're feeling for good. He uses all things for good; God is a God of redemption and healing. Ask Him to draw near to you tonight so when morning dawns, you will face the day with gladness and an earnest spirit.

When hope is in your heart and the unfailing love of God is on your side, you can conquer anything. Cling to that promise tonight; God is with you wherever you go.

*Therefore let us draw near with confidence to
the throne of grace, so that we may receive mercy
and find grace to help in time of need.*
HEBREWS 4:16 NASB

*From the ends of the earth I call to you,
I call as my heart grows faint;
lead me to the rock that is higher than I.*
PSALM 61:2

*"What no eye has seen, what no ear has heard, and
what no human mind has conceived"—the things
God has prepared for those who love him.*
1 CORINTHIANS 2:9

Prayer

FATHER IN HEAVEN, YOU know the discouragement I am facing this evening. My spirit feels crushed and my heart is heavy; yet I know in my heart of hearts that You are God and You are good. I ask for Your Holy Spirit to come and overwhelm me with encouragement, because I believe Your love never disappoints. Come quickly, Lord Jesus.

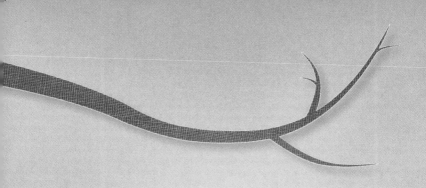

Blessing

MAY YOU FEEL AN
overwhelming sense of God's
hope permeating your spirit
tonight. As you approach the
Lord's throne, may you see
God for who He is—King
over your life—and worship
Him in gladness, for He is
doing a good work in you.

Praise

LORD, I PRAISE YOU BECAUSE
even in my darkest nights of
discouragement and disappointment,
You shine Your light of beauty
and majesty and hope into my life.
When I feel like giving up, You
remind me of the ways You have
blessed me and continue to work in
my life. Thank You for being my
constant companion, Father God.

God's Peace for When You Are Afraid of the Future

hen you think of the future, do you feel happy anticipation or nervous dread? Are you excited for what's to come, or do you fear what you cannot see? If you're lying awake, wondering what the future holds, afraid of what God may require of you or has planned for your life, be comforted. Be cheered! The Bible promises Jesus' followers there is hope for the future—the days to come are not to be feared. There are a few reasons for this great hope.

First, God promises you His presence. He assures you He is with you. Whether your future holds great joy or heartbreak, or some of both, the Lord is continually with you (Matthew 28:20). He is your guide and your refuge. He will never leave or forsake you. When you think of your future, remember this: circumstances may shift and change, but the Lord will be with you forever. He will never leave your side.

The Lord also says that He leads your way—He will guide you always and satisfy your needs (Isaiah 58:11). He promises to give you hope and future—He has plans to prosper you and not to harm you (Jeremiah 29:11).

Finally, when He looks at our future, God says that He will complete a good work in us (Philippians 1:6). Before

we were even growing in our mothers' wombs, He began weaving a story throughout our lives, and He will bring it to completion.

Friend, you don't need to be afraid of the future, and you can lie down in sweet peace tonight. Your heavenly Father isn't afraid, and He promises to be with you. He promises to lead you and to bring your story to completion in the best possible way. What a beautiful truth to cling to! When you fall asleep, you can rest knowing the Lord is holding you and your future in the palm of His hand.

Being confident of this, that he who began a good work in you
will carry it on to completion until the day of Christ Jesus.

PHILIPPIANS 1:6

Not that I have already obtained all this, or have already
arrived at my goal, but I press on to take hold of that for
which Christ Jesus took hold of me. Brothers and sisters, I
do not consider myself yet to have taken hold of it. But one
thing I do: Forgetting what is behind and straining toward
what is ahead, I press on toward the goal to win the prize
for which God has called me heavenward in Christ Jesus.

PHILIPPIANS 3:12–14

"For I know the plans I have for you," declares
the LORD, *"plans to prosper you and not to harm*
you, plans to give you hope and a future."

JEREMIAH 29:11

Prayer

WHEN I THINK OF MY future, Father God, I feel afraid. I don't know what's coming and I fear it may be too much to handle. But I choose to rest in Your great faithfulness tonight. Your Word promises that You will take care of me today, tomorrow, and through eternity; when I feel weak, remind me of that truth.

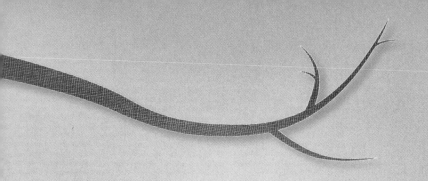

Blessing

IN EVERY STEP OF YOUR
life's path, may you feel the
Lord's steady and gentle hand
leading you. May you rejoice
in His blessings along the
way and revel in His presence
every moment of the day.

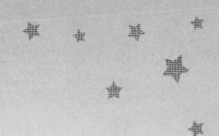

Praise

ALMIGHTY GOD, YOU ARE
Lord of the future, yet You dwell
with me in every moment of the
day and night. Thank You for Your
guiding hand; even when I am
afraid or fearful of the next step,
Your Word tells me my fear is
for naught. I praise You, Maker of
my future and God over my life.

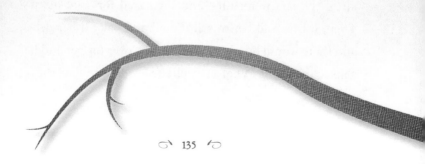

God's Peace for When You Are Anxious About Money

*I*s the thought of money keeping you awake right now? If so, you're not the only one. Medical bills, mortgage payments, college tuition, retirement funds, grocery money, car repairs—these all require money, and they are realities in many of our lives. Whether an unexpected bill, sudden job loss, or the reality of barely scraping by is on your mind tonight, may you feel the peace of God flood your soul, for He provides for His children in mysterious, perfect, and loving ways.

Do you remember the story of Elisha and the widow (2 Kings 4:1–7)? The widow had no money, her husband left a massive amount of debt, and his creditor was threatening to take her sons for payment. Instead of raining money from the sky, God provided for her in a truly unique way. Elisha told her to go and ask her neighbors for empty jars and then pour oil into each jar. The oil kept flowing until all of the jars were full—and she asked for a lot of jars! Then, Elisha told her to sell the oil and pay off her debts, and there would be enough money left over for her and her sons to live off of. What a story! The Lord multiplied the oil

for the widow—and in providing through a rather obscure way, the widow and her sons were blessed abundantly.

As you lie awake, stressed about providing for yourself or your family, feeling burdened by the overwhelming sensation of not having "enough," reflect on the truths in God's Word instead of the worries in your mind. He may not provide for you in the exact way you expect, but His way will always be good, and it will always be enough.

In Philippians, Paul said God will meet your every need (Philippians 4:19), and Jesus also said the Father loves to give good gifts to His children (Matthew 7:11). If you are a parent or have a special child in your life, reflect on the love you feel for him or her. You would do anything to satiate their needs, and you would probably go above and beyond. That is how the Lord is with His followers. That is how He feels about you.

Rest your head on your pillow, trusting that your Provider loves you like a father loves his children. Remember what the Lord has done for you in the past, and know that He is still with you now and in the future.

"Therefore I say to you, all things for which you
pray and ask, believe that you have received
them, and they will be granted you."

MARK 11:24 NASB

My God will supply all your needs according
to His riches in glory in Christ Jesus.

PHILIPPIANS 4:19 NASB

"Look at the birds of the air; they do not sow or reap or
store away in barns, and yet your heavenly Father feeds
them. Are you not much more valuable than they?"

MATTHEW 6:26

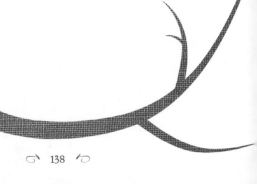

Prayer

LORD, I FEEL SO ANXIOUS
tonight about having enough
money. Help me trust that You
are faithful to Your children
and will provide for my every
need. Give me strength to look
heavenward toward You instead
of at my bank account, for
ultimately You are my provider.

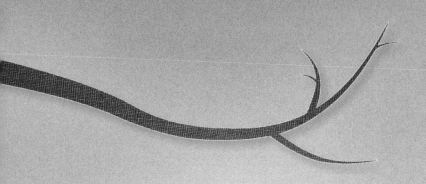

Blessing

MAY GOD'S PROMISES OF
provision give you peace
tonight. May you fall asleep
with a contented heart,
knowing He will provide
everything you need, in His
time and in His perfect way.

Praise

LORD, I PRAISE YOU FOR
the promises in Your Word.
Thank You for making it so
clear in Scripture that You
will always meet my needs.
I am so grateful for Your
constant care and attention,
and lift my heart in gratitude
for all Your good gifts.

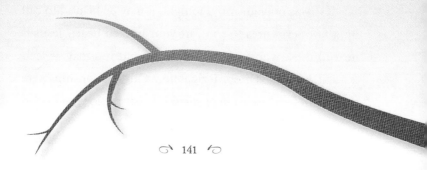

God's Peace for When You Are Grieving a Lost Relationship

*I*n this broken world, relationships can get messy. Whether it's between a parent and child, boyfriend and girlfriend, grandparent and grandchild, stepmother and stepchild, husband and wife, teacher and student, or among coworkers, relationships are at the core of our lives—and sometimes, when they aren't as they should be, they bring us grief and sorrow.

Are you grieving a relationship that has deteriorated? Whether it dissolved in a long, tangled mess over the years or conflict erupted out of nowhere, broken relationships hurt. Maybe it felt good to get out of that relationship then, but now, as you lie awake staring at the ceiling, regret begins seeping into your bones. Maybe you long for reconciliation, but it hasn't come—even after years of praying. Dear child, it is grievous when our actions caused a broken bridge or when those we love don't respond to our outreached hand.

If this is on your mind tonight, it may be helpful to call up a few Scriptures to comfort your broken heart. Jesus is near to those who are brokenhearted, and you may be feeling a little crushed in spirit right now. Our relationships were not meant for dissension or sorrow or frustration, and when

brokenness captures our relationships, it feels devastating and wrong. Your heart feels like it may never be repaired. Beloved, Jesus is with you. He heals the brokenhearted. He binds the open wounds that bring on such pain. He is healer not just of the body, but also of the spirit. Cry out to Him in your sorrow—He surely hears you.

In the quiet of tonight, be comforted: the Lord remembers you. He is the God of all comfort and the healer of fragmented, devastated, tender hearts. Our Father is compassionate toward His children and He loves us so much He sent His only beloved Son to die—so that He could have a redeemed relationship with us, *with you*. Be encouraged, dear one; the Lord hears you and your cries tonight. Even though Jesus no longer walks the streets of the earth, the Holy Spirit abides with us in all our need. Find solace and comfort in His compassion and reflect on the truth in His Word.

*Praise be to the God and Father of our Lord Jesus Christ,
the Father of compassion and the God of all comfort, who
comforts us in all our troubles, so that we can comfort those
in any trouble with the comfort we ourselves receive from
God. For just as we share abundantly in the sufferings of
Christ, so also our comfort abounds through Christ.*

2 CORINTHIANS 1:3–5

*But the Comforter, which is the Holy Ghost,
whom the Father will send in my name, he shall
teach you all things, and bring all things to your
remembrance, whatsoever I have said unto you.*

JOHN 14:26 KJV

*The LORD is close to the brokenhearted
and saves those who are crushed in spirit.*

PSALM 34:18

Prayer

JESUS, FRIEND OF SINNERS, I am grieved by the loss of my relationship. My heart cries out in sadness and longing, but I know in the midst of my grief, You are with me. You are always at the eye of the storm, offering calm amidst calamity; as I try to fall asleep this evening, tend to me gently.

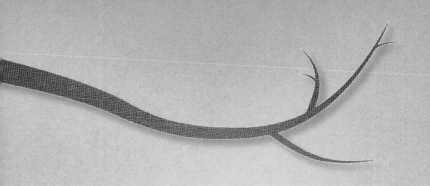

Blessing

MAY YOU TRULY

experience the comfort of God
the Father, the love of Jesus
the Son, and the communion
of the Holy Spirit as you
grieve your lost relationship.
May your sorrow be turned
to dancing as you think on
the goodness of the Lord.

Praise

LORD, EVEN WHEN I AM
downcast, I praise You—
my comfort and strength.
You are a God to be
praised, even when I'm
filled with grief. Thank
You for Your steadfastness,
my precious Lord.

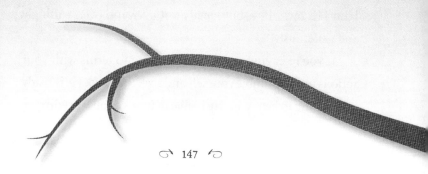

God's Peace for When You Feel Guilty

*I*t's always tough to sleep when feeling guilty, isn't it? The snide remark during the meeting, the way you snapped at your mom on the phone, the glare you bestowed on your spouse, the frustration that spilled out when the kids asked one too many questions. You may have felt a moment of relief for a second, but now, as you're trying to fall asleep, you feel a tremendous amount of guilt.

Even though your kids, parents, spouse, coworker, or anyone else you offended today might be sleeping at this hour, the Lord is not sleeping. He is waiting for you to ask for forgiveness—not just because He's a perfect God, but also because it will make you feel so much better. Asking for forgiveness acknowledges that you were wrong and restores brokenness in relationships. Grace is heaped upon your head and mercy is poured on your feet as the Lord washes you clean with His own forgiveness. That forgiveness comes from the blood He shed on the cross; it was not free—it cost Him His own life—but He gives it over and over, willingly and generously.

If you're having a hard time coming to terms with your actions today, humble yourself and seek the Lord. He is ready and willing to hear you. He is able to forgive you. He will give

you strength for a new day filled with new mercies and new grace. As you seek God's face, ask Him to give you words to right the situation tomorrow. It doesn't need to be anything elaborate or eloquent—just come before that person with humility of heart. Two simple words—I'm sorry—will cleanse you of the burden of guilt you are carrying.

Now, with the Lord's full forgiveness and a newfound humility, you can go to sleep tonight being filled with peace instead of regret. Guilt no longer holds its power over you tonight; let your body sink into your mattress with a renewed feeling of joy and the liberty of a clean conscience. You can fall asleep with a smile on your face and a sweet song in your heart, for the Lord has forgiven you of your transgressions—He has freed you of your sin. Go and sleep now in peace, beloved. Your sins have been forgiven.

Be kind and compassionate to one another, forgiving
each other, just as in Christ God forgave you.

EPHESIANS 4:32

As far as the east is from the west,
so far has he removed our transgressions from us.

PSALM 103:12

If we confess our sins, he is faithful and just and will forgive
us our sins and purify us from all unrighteousness.

1 JOHN 1:9

Prayer

FORGIVE ME, LORD. I HAVE sinned today and need to ask for Your forgiveness. Please take away my guilt and wipe my slate clean with the blood of Jesus Christ, of which I am so unworthy. I am a sinner in need of my Savior.

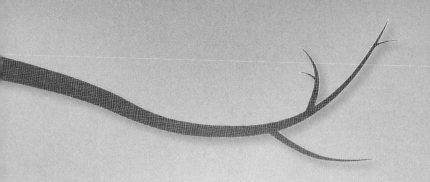

Blessing

MAY YOU EXPERIENCE THE
quick forgiveness of the Lord and
bestow His generosity on others as
you go about your day tomorrow.
May you find strength to be slow
to anger—and when you find
yourself needing forgiveness,
may you ask for it freely, and
may it be given to you freely.

Praise

THANK YOU FOR

removing my sins from me,
O Lord, and for no longer
remembering them. It is a
tremendous blessing to have
Your forgiveness and grace,
heavenly Father. I praise You;
You are quick to forgive, slow
to anger, and rich in love.

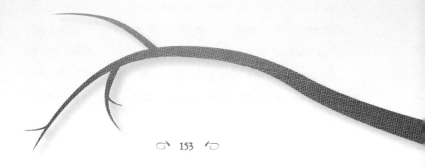

God's Peace for When You Feel Lonely

*L*oneliness can happen with or without anyone around. You can feel lonely in the middle of a crowd of people at Union Station or alone in your bedroom with nothing but the sight of headlights shining through your curtains. You may have just gone through a breakup, become an empty nester, or moved to a different city. Loneliness has affected us all at some point in our lives, and it's often a recurring theme.

If you're feeling lonely tonight—the house is just a little too quiet, the silence is a little too loud—take a few moments to think about these truths . . .

You have a Maker who will never leave you or forsake you. It can be hard to believe that because our Lord is invisible, but rest assured: if you ask, He will make Himself known in tangible ways. Believe it or not, the Lord knows what loneliness is like. While He was breathing life into Adam's body, He said, "It is not good for the man to be alone. I will make a helper suitable for him." And thus, Eve was created. We were created for intimacy with other people, for contact and communion with other human beings.

When we don't have a community, when we lack someone we can turn to in the toughest times, when we feel the

absence of a spouse or a child or a parent, loneliness tends to feel overwhelming. It's normal. And dear friend, you can cry out to the Lord in your loneliness, asking Him to bring people into your life to help form a community of loved ones. It's not good for man or woman to be alone.

Yet, in the silent hours of the night, even when we feel alone, we are never really alone. Because of our relationship with God, we have holy communion with the Father, the Son, and the Holy Spirit at all times. We are known and loved in that relationship. We are cherished. You are cherished. Even if you are feeling the deep pangs of loneliness tonight, you can rest assured that you are loved, you are known, and you are complete in Him. Find solace in the Most High King tonight—the One who sits above all, yet utterly adores you and wants to abide with you in your loneliest hours.

Turn to me and have mercy on me,
because I am lonely and hurting.
My troubles have grown larger;
free me from my problems.

PSALM 25:16–17 NCV

"Surely I am with you always, to the very end of the age."

MATTHEW 28:20

When he calls to me, I will answer him;
I will be with him in trouble;
I will rescue him and honor him.

PSALM 91:15 ESV

Prayer

TONIGHT, I FEEL SO isolated and alone. I need Your presence to satisfy me, Lord. It is hard to feel as though I'm not on my own, and I'm lying awake with an overwhelming sense of loneliness. Come quickly to me, Lord Jesus. I need You.

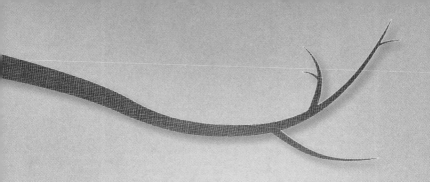

Blessing

MAY YOU BE DELIGHTED

and satisfied by the presence
of God this very evening.
May His Spirit provide
great comfort for you, both
tonight and in the future.
You are so loved; may you
experience His strong and
steady arms in a tangible way.

Praise

THANK YOU, FATHER,
for coming to the aid of Your
child. Thank You, Jesus, for
Your promise to never leave
or forsake me. And thank
You, Holy Spirit, for being
my comforter and friend.

God's Peace for When You Are Dissatisfied

*D*eep breaths in and out, in and out. As you desperately try to fall asleep, it's of no avail—you're awake, and you know sleep just won't come easily tonight. Your body is tired, but your mind and heart keep running on the hamster wheel of discontentment. You feel so unsatisfied right now—and you keep thinking, *If only I could have that . . . then I'd feel better*. What is it you want, dear friend? A new job, a renovated kitchen, a newer car, calmer kids, or a transformed body? The list goes on.

Here is the truth: you might be happier with those things. But that happiness is fleeting—so fleeting. For possessions, careers, even people cannot fill the God-sized gap we hold in our hearts. Only the Lord can fill that incessant craving you're feeling right now. You might feel completely confident in the one thing you're hoping for, but the Bible tells us and experience points to the fact that nothing in this world can complete us like God can.

If you're feeling dissatisfied in an area of your life right now, confess that to the Hearer of your prayers. He knows that you are struggling and knows your turmoil within, but He wants you to communicate it to Him. Discontentment is not an easy thing to triumph over. In fact, it's something that

many people struggle with on a daily basis. This is because we are constantly tempted to satisfy our souls in our own way, in our own power. Friend, rest assured tonight that the Lord desires for you to be content, no matter what is happening in your life, but He wants to be the One to satisfy you. He knows what we need and want before we do!

No matter what area you are discontent in, the Lord is ready to meet you there. If you are feeling frustrated with your family life, voice those frustrations to Him. He understands. Jesus grew up with brothers during His time here on earth. Or if you're discontent with your home, ask God to fill you with gratitude for what you do have, and to show you ways to make it a home you can enjoy and appreciate. If you feel lonely and desire a relationship, ask the Lord to fill that empty space within your heart. Ultimately, He is the *only* One who can rescue you from the mire of discontentment. Instead of getting caught in the web of comparison, jealousy, or restlessness, collapse at the foot of the cross. It's where healing, satisfaction, and joy come. You can find rest for your soul there, and, still tonight, you can find rest for your body too.

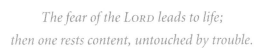

*The fear of the L*ORD *leads to life;*
then one rests content, untouched by trouble.

PROVERBS 19:23

Keep your lives free from the love of money and be
content with what you have, because God has said,
"Never will I leave you; never will I forsake you."

HEBREWS 13:5

May the words of my mouth
and the meditation of my heart
be pleasing to you,
*O L*ORD, *my rock and my redeemer.*

PSALM 19:14 NLT

"Call to Me, and I will answer you, and show you
great and mighty things, which you do not know."

JEREMIAH 33:3 NKJV

Prayer

LORD, IT'S TOUGH TO LIVE in a world where dissatisfaction is so prevalent. It's hard for me to find true rest in You, and tonight I am so tired of being discontent; I am tired of yearning for that one more thing I am craving, because it will never satisfy. Lead me to Your resting place, to the rock that is higher than I. I know it's the only place I will find true contentment.

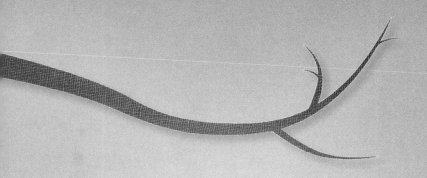

Blessing

DEAR CHILD OF GOD, MAY
you be filled to the brim
with the joy of the Lord.
May you be captivated by His
love for you and enthralled
with the riches He brings
you each and every day.

Praise

I PRAISE YOU, LORD, FOR
I am fearfully and wonderfully
made. You created me to yearn
for You and the things of Your
kingdom, not the trappings
of this earth. Thank You for
reminding me of that again
and again and for the grace
You extend when I stumble.

God's Peace for When You Are Weary

*W*as today another one of those days when everything seemed to go wrong? From the moment you woke up until your head hit the pillow, it just seemed like the world was against you once again, and you were all on your own to face the obstacles. Frustrating events and feelings piled up day by day, brick by brick, until you were staring at a wall seemingly impossible to scale. And now, as you try to drift into sleep, your shoulders still feel burdened by all those bricks.

We live in a broken world. Life can be utterly discouraging sometimes. The joy and peace that we are given by Christ can easily be overshadowed by difficult circumstances, and it can be so hard to scale the wall of weariness. Now as you're lying sleepless while the seconds, minutes, and hours tick by, you're wondering if sleep will ever come. Discouragement mounts as rest fails you, and you begin replaying everything that happened to lead to this dark place, concentrating on the hardest moments.

Oh, dear friend, discouragement is such a hard state in which to rest. It's wearisome, heavy, and often so lonely. It drains your spirit and robs you of hope. If you're in that place this evening, here is some encouragement for you—straight

from God's Word. Imagine all those bricks, everything that is weighing you down, falling off one by one into a dusty, piled-up heap at the foot of the cross. Jesus promised us an easy yoke and a light burden because of His work on the cross; that means that even when we're discouraged, we can still rest—*in Him*.

Instead of tossing and turning all night and panicking about how exhausted you might feel tomorrow, try to reflect on the strength and peace God offers when you feel weary and worn. It is there for your taking. Be comforted, because you are not alone in your discouragement and it is not uncommon in the Christian life. In fact, Scripture says that you will grow tired and weary—but when your hope is in the Lord, He will help you through it. Even though you are afflicted and perplexed, you don't need to be driven to despair, for the King of hope is holding out His arms, ready to embrace you as the wall of weariness transforms into a renewed spirit.

*He gives strength to the weary
and increases the power of the weak.
Even youths grow tired and weary,
and young men stumble and fall;
but those who hope in the Lord
will renew their strength.
They will soar on wings like eagles;
they will run and not grow weary,
they will walk and not be faint.*

ISAIAH 40:29–31

*I lay down and slept;
I woke again, for the Lord sustained me.*

PSALM 3:5 ESV

*"Have I not commanded you? Be strong and courageous.
Do not be afraid; do not be discouraged, for the Lord
your God will be with you wherever you go."*

JOSHUA 1:9

*Why are you cast down, O my soul,
and why are you in turmoil within me?
Hope in God; for I shall again praise him,
my salvation and my God.*

PSALM 43:5 ESV

Prayer

LIFE HAS BEEN SO HARD, Lord. Help me to give You my burdens and take on Your joy and peace tonight. Give me a light heart and a sound night of sleep.

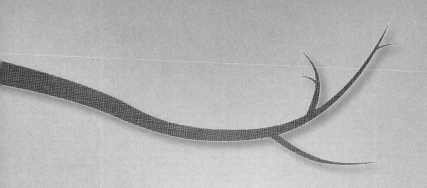

Blessing

MAY YOUR WEARINESS

and heaviness be turned
to peace that passes all
understanding. Even now,
as you are in the dark of
night, may your face be
pointed toward the light
of hope the Lord gives.

Praise

I PRAISE YOU, JESUS, FOR
allowing me to lay my
burdens at the foot of the
cross. Thank You for caring
for me so much and for
making my burden light.

God's Peace for When Your Heart Feels Broken

*S*adness can strike in the most peculiar of moments, and it often hits in the middle of the night. You're lying in bed, trying to fall asleep, and your heart just feels broken. It's not like hunger, where you can satisfy the pangs with a bowl of cereal or a late-night bag of popcorn; sadness is an emotion, and sometimes it's there to stay for the duration of your evening.

Are you feeling sad tonight? Are you tired of feeling like your heart is broken? But when you try to sleep, you stare at the ceiling with tears rolling down your face, drenching your pillow? Take heart—the Lord is with you. He knows your sadness. He knows where it came from, He knows how much pain your heart is in, and He knows what you need.

If you're sad and deeply lonely tonight, lean on the Lord. You don't need to pray the feeling away; just ask your loving Father to abide with you in your sadness, in the darkness, in the heaviness. He never leaves His children, and He certainly will hear you when you call. God may not take your sadness away, but He promises to be with you in your darkest hour. You may recognize the words of the hymn "Abide with Me," written more than a century ago. These words

ring true even today, and especially this evening, for you. The hymnist Henry F. Lyte wrote:

> Abide with me! Fast falls the eventide;
> The darkness deepens; Lord, with me abide.
> When other helpers fail and comforts flee,
> Help of the helpless, oh, abide with me.

As you begin to pray, ask God to comfort you with His presence. Ask Him to make Himself known to you. Even if you can barely speak because tears are thick in your throat, know that the Holy Spirit is interceding for you, and God hears your prayers with a kind and compassionate heart. Your Savior knows sadness. He felt grieved when His friend Lazarus died and He felt sad when He knew His disciple Judas was going to betray Him with a kiss. When you pour out your sadness to Jesus, He knows exactly how it feels—and you are not alone.

Rest in that knowledge tonight. The tears might continue to fall, your heart may still feel like it's breaking, but your Lord Jesus is so close to you.

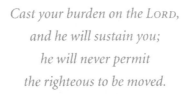

Cast your burden on the LORD,
and he will sustain you;
he will never permit
the righteous to be moved.

PSALM 55:22 ESV

For he has not despised or abhorred
the affliction of the afflicted,
and he has not hidden his face from him,
but has heard, when he cried to him.

PSALM 22:24 ESV

You have kept count of my tossings;
put my tears in your bottle.
Are they not in your book?

PSALM 56:8 ESV

It is of the Lord's mercies that we are not
consumed, because his compassions fail not.
They are new every morning: great is thy faithfulness.

LAMENTATIONS 3:22–23 KJV

Prayer

LORD, LIKE THE HYMNIST wrote, I need You to abide with me. The evening has come and nothing but Your presence will comfort me. You are helper of the helpless, strength of the weak, and comforter to the mourning; oh, abide with me.

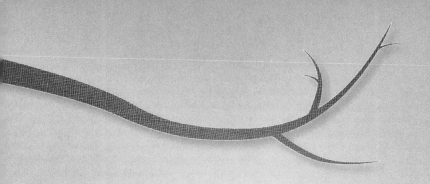

Blessing

MAY YOU FEEL THE ALL-
encompassing presence of the
Lord throughout all the hours
of the night. May you drift
into a deep sleep, comforted
by Jesus' promises and love.

Praise

DEAR JESUS, I PRAISE

You that You're with me in
my darkest times. Thank
You for coming to my rescue
and giving me the gift of
Your presence tonight.

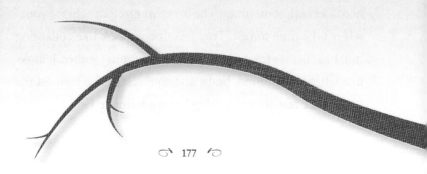

God's Peace for When You Are Anxious About Tomorrow

*A*s you sink into bed tonight, exhausted, are you already thinking about tomorrow's meetings, next week's obligations, next month's deadlines? You're anxious about tomorrow . . . and the next day . . . and the next. Whether you're a busy mom who's worried about your child's future, an overwhelmed college student in the throes of midterms, or a rising executive with demands pulling from every direction, it's difficult not knowing what tomorrow will bring. This anxiety is something that keeps many people awake at night—but does it do any good?

One result of anxiety is that it can certainly make you feel productive. At least you're keeping a running tally in your mind of things to do, scenarios that could go wrong, or new ideas to explore, right? But the problem is this: you can't keep going all the time. Your mind and body need a break. You need a break. Your boss needs a break. Even the president needs a break sometimes. The best thing you can do for yourself is take time to rest. True rest doesn't look like collapsing into bed, nerves fried and adrenaline pumping, either. It looks like letting your mind, body, and soul rest in the palm of the Lord. True rest always involves surrendering to God.

God doesn't tell us to rest for His own good—He tells us to rest for *our* own good. God worked six days and rested the seventh. He was—and is—the mastermind behind the entire world, yet He took time to give Himself a break. To cease from working, to cease from creating, cease from *doing*.

Emulate the Lord's pattern of work and rest tonight. While you are in bed you can't work efficiently and you certainly can't get anything done. Nighttime calls for rest. There may be unforeseen challenges ahead tomorrow, and there might be things that have been left undone today. But the Lord tells us not to worry about tomorrow because each day has enough trouble of its own (Matthew 6:34). Sink into your bed letting a wave of relief wash over you; tomorrow is not yet here. You have nothing on your agenda right now except for sleep.

Ask the Lord to lift the burden of anxiety off your shoulders. As sure as the stars twinkling in the night sky, He will answer your request. As gently as the crickets sing throughout the evening, the Lord will come to you. Rest tonight, dear one. The Lord is near.

*Do not be anxious about anything, but in
every situation, by prayer and petition, with
thanksgiving, present your requests to God.*

PHILIPPIANS 4:6

*Cast your cares on the LORD and he will sustain you;
he will never let the righteous be shaken.*

PSALM 55:22

*When the righteous cry for help, the LORD hears
and delivers them out of all their troubles.*

PSALM 34:17 ESV

*"But in the seventh year there shall be a Sabbath of
solemn rest for the land, a Sabbath to the Lord. You
shall not sow your field or prune your vineyard."*

LEVITICUS 25:4 ESV

Prayer

I COME TO YOU WITH A troubled, anxious heart, Lord. I ask You now to take away my anxiety and fear so that I can rest deeply tonight. Please answer my prayer quickly!

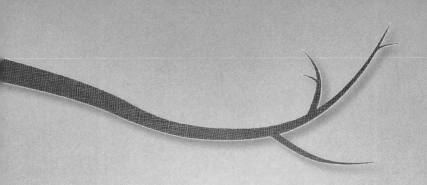

Blessing

MAY YOU FEEL THE ALL-
encompassing peace of the
Lord tonight, filling your
spirit with complete trust and
your body with rest. May the
always-faithful God take your
anxieties and worries, giving
you a night of sweet sleep.

Praise

I PRAISE YOU, MY JESUS,
for knowing just what I need.
Thank You for always being
here when my fears need to
be eased and my anxiety needs
to be stilled; I am so grateful
You have never given up on
me but continue to be my El
Shaddai, my all-sufficient One.

God's Peace for When You Can't Stop Worrying

Worrying. Everyone struggles with it at one point or another. Are you worrying right now? So much, in fact, that you can't fall into a peaceful slumber? We have all been there. We worry about world events. We worry about how others perceive us, how we're going to pay that bill, how we're going to find more hours in the day. We worry about the next day, the next month, even five years down the road. We are expert worriers. However, worrying is something God talks about many times in Scripture; as humans, we are prone to worry, but the Lord clearly tells us not to.

When Jesus talks about worry in the Bible, He doesn't just say not to worry about clothes or food—He says not to be anxious about *anything*. He tells us not to worry about our lives. Instead, we are to seek God's kingdom, and everything else will be provided for us because the Lord knows what we need.

Tonight, try turning your worry into worship. You may not know the answers or the outcome of your problems or struggles, but you know the One who does. If you're able to turn your mind from worrying into worshipping the Most

High King, you will finally feel your shoulders relax. Your brow will unfurrow and your hands will slowly unclench themselves. Jesus tells us we cannot add a single day to our lives by worrying. Listen to your Savior; He knows what is best.

As you lie back down on your pillow and worry creeps back in, begin worshipping the Lord. Praise Him for His faithfulness, exalt Him for answered prayers, rejoice in the suffering He redeemed. Think back through your day: what were the small ways He showed up? The sunset that took your breath away, your child's tight hug, an unexpected letter from a far-off friend, an affirmation from your boss—there are countless ways He has blessed you today. As you practice a heart of gratitude, you will find that your heart feels lighter and more joyful. It's as it should be.

You can't control many of your circumstances; you don't know the future or have all the answers. But you have a God who clothes flowers in beauty and provides food for the tiny sparrows. You serve a mighty, holy, yet wholly intimate God. Let your soul be flooded with peace; you are in good hands.

Cast all your anxiety on him because he cares for you.

1 Peter 5:7

*Trust in the Lord with all your heart
and lean not on your own understanding;
in all your ways submit to him,
and he will make your paths straight.*

Proverbs 3:5–6

Prayer

I AM PRONE TO WORRY,
Father. Even when I decide not
to worry, it's a slippery trap that
I somehow fall into so easily.
Remind me to turn my worry into
worship and keep my eyes fixed
on You and Your good gifts.

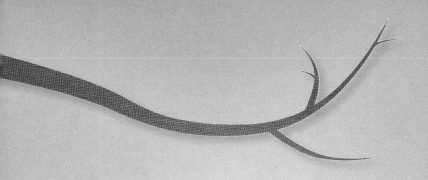

Blessing

CHILD OF THE KING,
may your eyes be opened
to the small miracles God
performs each day in your
life; may your mind be full
of worship and may you
flee from worry, straight
into the arms of Jesus.

Praise

YOU KNOW HOW I
struggle with worry, Lord, and
I thank You for Your daily
deliverance. You continually
remind me to seek Your face
and Your kingdom; even when I
am deeply entrenched in the pit
of worry, You rescue me. I praise
You for Your patience with me
and for Your eternal goodness.

God's Peace for When Your Prayers Aren't Answered

*A*ll around you, people are sleeping. The lights in the house next door are out, and even the birds have ceased their singing. But not you. Your mind is full of questions and concerns, worries, and doubts. The reason? Your prayers aren't being answered—at least, not that you see. So instead of sleeping, you're up, pacing the house, wondering why God is seemingly ignoring your requests, trying to make sense of it all. Are you not praying enough? Are you praying too much? Is what you're asking not in His will? Is God testing your faith? There are so many questions, but no answers to speak of, no writing on the wall.

Know that you are not the only one who struggles with wondering why your prayers aren't being answered. We serve a great and mighty God, but often His ways are so mysterious and our minds are so futile we get discouraged and frustrated. Does this sound familiar to you?

I urge you, friend—don't give up. Jesus tells us to ask, seek, and knock. And it's important to keep on asking and knocking, even when God seems silent. His silence doesn't mean He isn't listening and working on our behalf, because He is—in ways we can't even conceive. There are also times

when His answer is wait. Or sometimes the answer is no. These answers make it especially difficult to believe that God really loves us! But we must trust that His "wait" and "no" are because He loves us *so* much that He has a better answer to situations than what our limited minds can fathom. It's so important to believe and cling to the depths of His love and not get discouraged.

Tonight, even if you aren't necessarily feeling that God is at work in your life, you can be assured that He is indeed working. Scripture tells us our God never sleeps, and that He is faithful to His people. In this very moment, He is carrying out a perfect, heaven-orchestrated story for your life and for the lives of those you love. He's not working in a general way—He's working in an intricate, personalized way. He is near and hears your prayers.

Keep your eyes open for little glimpses of answers and encouragement throughout each day. They'll come. They might not come tonight—but that's okay. Tonight, it's time to rest. Go to sleep reciting God's Word and promises. He will hear every word.

*This is the confidence we have in approaching God:
that if we ask anything according to his will, he hears
us. And if we know that he hears us—whatever we
ask—we know that we have what we asked of him.*

1 JOHN 5:14–15

*"Call to me and I will answer you and tell you great
and unsearchable things you do not know."*

JEREMIAH 33:3

*"Ask and it will be given to you; seek and you will
find; knock and the door will be opened to you. For
everyone who asks receives; the one who seeks finds;
and to the one who knocks, the door will be opened."*

MATTHEW 7:7–8

Prayer

LORD, YOU KNOW HOW disappointed and frustrated I am right now. I feel as if my prayers are not being answered, and it's very discouraging. But I'm leaning on Scripture, which says if I call on You, the Hearer of my prayers, You will answer. Please give me patience and perseverance even in the face of unanswered prayer; help me not to lose heart.

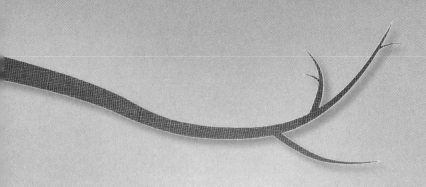

Blessing

EVEN IN THE MIDST OF
unanswered prayer, may you
stand strong in your faith,
knowing God is perfect, loving,
mysterious, and good. May
God be quick to comfort you
when your frustration and
discouragement overwhelms
your soul, and may you find
peace and joy in serving Him
even when you don't understand.

Praise

FATHER, THANK YOU FOR
being so intimately involved in
my life. You are a great God,
and even though my mind can't
fully wrap around Your ways,
I know You are working all
things together for good. Thank
You for Your good work in my
life and for hearing my prayers.

God's Peace for When You Are Awake for No Reason

*O*n some nights, it's so easy to fall asleep. Your head hits the pillow, and before you know it, your alarm clock is blaring. But other nights, like tonight, you don't have that luxury. Instead, you're awake. Surfing the Web, watching mindless TV; everyone is asleep except for you, it seems.

Sometimes we're awake for no reason. We don't feel particularly stressed. We feel relatively relaxed and joyful. We feel pretty content in life. And we didn't drink any espresso before bed. But sleep, it is ever elusive. Do you have that right now? Often when you're awake for no reason, it can be easy to become discouraged or anxious. Discouraged because you're awake again, or anxious because you know your mind and body need rest.

Instead of focusing on that, dear friend, think on this: you have some extra time to be alone with the Lord right now. Why not make the most of it? As you sit up in bed or tiptoe through your quiet house, bring to mind different ways the Lord has sustained you throughout the day or week. Have you felt His presence in times when you felt utterly weak? Has He blessed you with any surprises? Have

you seen Him work in the lives of those closest to you? As you reflect on God's goodness, let your heart rejoice. He has done great things for you!

Now is the perfect time to spend time praising Him or coming to the Lord with matters of the heart. It's a wonderful time to intercede in prayer for friends, family, and coworkers who might be struggling in some way. Yes, the hours of the night are meant for sleeping, but as you try to sleep, time is not wasted if you're communing with the Lord.

The busyness of the day can be quite demanding; you have work to tend to, children to love, relationships to uphold, and commitments to maintain. There are meetings and lunches and decisions that tend to captivate your mind most of the day. Yet, the late evening hours spent alone are some of the sweetest times with the Lord. Nothing is distracting; no emails are popping up on your phone and no children are vying for your attention. Take advantage of this time. Take a few moments with your heavenly Father. He is always up for a late-night chat.

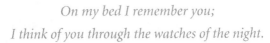

On my bed I remember you;
I think of you through the watches of the night.

PSALM 63:6

Arise, cry out in the night,
as the watches of the night begin;
pour out your heart like water
in the presence of the Lord.

LAMENTATIONS 2:19

I call out to the LORD,
and he answers me from his holy mountain.
I lie down and sleep;
I wake again, because the LORD sustains me.

PSALM 3:4–5

Return to your rest, my soul,
for the LORD has been good to you.

PSALM 116:7

You keep him in perfect peace
whose mind is stayed on you,
because he trusts in you.
Trust in the LORD forever,
for the LORD GOD is an everlasting rock.

ISAIAH 26:3–4 ESV

Prayer

THANK YOU THAT I CAN come to You at any time of day or night, O Lord. You are a God who never slumbers or sleeps, and right now, I am unable to sleep. I want to take this time and reflect on Your goodness to me; help me commune with You in the quiet hours of this night.

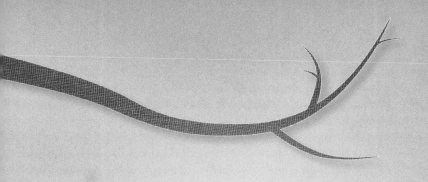

Blessing

MAY YOU HAVE A SWEET,
memorable time with the Lord
this evening. Even though sleep
has not yet come, your Father
God is ready and willing to
abide with you; He is eager
to hear your thoughts and
requests and praises. May you
take advantage of these still
hours and revel in the presence
of the Lord your God.

Praise

WHENEVER I SEEK YOUR
face, Lord, You answer me. I
praise You for Your constant
attention on my life. In these
late hours of the night, I
am filled with gratitude for
all that You have done in
my life. Your goodness is
especially apparent tonight—
all praise be to You, my God!